W9-BAA-970

THE GROLIER STUDENT ENCYCLOPEDIA OF
ENDANGERED SPECIES

 Grolier Educational Corporation
SHERMAN TURNPIKE, DANBURY, CONNECTICUT 06816

GROLIER EDUCATIONAL CORPORATION

Remmel Nunn, Vice President and Publisher
Robert R. Hall, Senior Vice President, Sales
Beverly A. Balaz, Vice President, Marketing
Laraine Balk, Vice President, Operations
Molly Stratton, Editor, New Reference Titles

THE GROLIER STUDENT ENCYCLOPEDIA OF ENDANGERED SPECIES

Remmel Nunn, Project Director
Shelby Rosenberg, Text and Layout Design
Diane Chando Frenick, Editor
Claudia Durrell, Cover Designer
M.E. Aslett Corporation, Electronic Production

Printed and bound in the United States of America.
Cataloging information provided separately at no charge,
and further cataloging information or electronic data disks
may be obtained from the Grolier Educational Corporation.

TABLE OF CONTENTS
VOLUME VI

HOW TO USE THIS VOLUME

The Grolier Student Encyclopedia of Endangered Species is designed to be a user-friendly guide to endangered animals of the world. In meeting this end, there are several features that require introduction so that the reader may obtain the full benefits of this unique encyclopedia.

ALPHABETICAL ORDER: *The Grolier Student Encyclopedia of Endangered Species* is organized alphabetically by common animal names rather than specific names. For example, if you are interested in researching the Red Wolf, it can be found under Wolf, Red. For easy finding when thumbing through the pages, the word wolf appears in the upper corner of the pages that include information on the Red Wolf. The same is true of all animals included in the encyclopedia.

This type of ordering was chosen for several reasons. First, animals of the same family are kept close together so that the reader need not look far when researching animals of the same type. The Dhole Wolf, for example, is only a page turn away from the Red Wolf. Second, for indexing purposes, this organization allows the reader to see, at a glance, the extent to which animals of a certain type are endangered. For example, if you wish to know what deer are in danger, simply turn to *D*, and a complete list of those deer included in the encyclopedia appears before you.

WHAT IS AN ENDANGERED SPECIES?

"Endangerment" is not defined by numbers. It is true that many endangered animals exist in low numbers. However, many animals that exist in large populations are endangered because certain factors in their environments are working against them, harming the animals' ability to survive. Such factors might include pollution, overcrowding, competition with other animal species, or a host of other factors presented throughout this series. By the same token, a species that exists only in small numbers may be thriving in its environment because no forces are working against it. While this species may be considered rare, it is not necessarily endangered. And while another species may number in the thousands, it may in fact be on its way to extinction.

INTRODUCTORY LOGOS: Each article begins with a colorful logo that serves as a quick summary of the endangered animal's vital statistics. Each logo contains the animal's common name, its scientific name, its endangerment code as determined by the IUCN (International Union for Conservation of Nature and Natural Resources), a map outlining the animal's area of distribution and home continent, and a color code that classifies the animal as a mammal, bird, reptile, or amphibian.

COLOR CODES: Each of the four animal types represented in the encyclopedia — mammal, bird, reptile, and amphibian — can be easily identified by the color code that classifies them. You will note that each animal's introductory logo is presented in one of four color schemes. This allows you, at a glance, to determine what type of animal you are reading about. The color codes are as follows:

▶ Mammal – purple/pink
▶ Bird – red/peach
▶ Reptile – green/yellow
▶ Amphibian – blue

MAPS: Each article in *The Grolier Student Encyclopedia of Endangered Species* is supplemented with a map highlighting the endangered animal's current area of distribution. The maps are vividly colored and shaded red in the area(s) where the animal lives. At the bottom of each map is a listing of continents, with the animal's home continent highlighted. This helps the reader to see the extent of the animal's specific distribution, as well as the larger area in which the animal lives.

GLOSSARY: A comprehensive glossary can be found in the last volume of the series. This glossary serves as a guide to terms that are important in understanding the subject matter of the articles.

Common Name

Latin Name

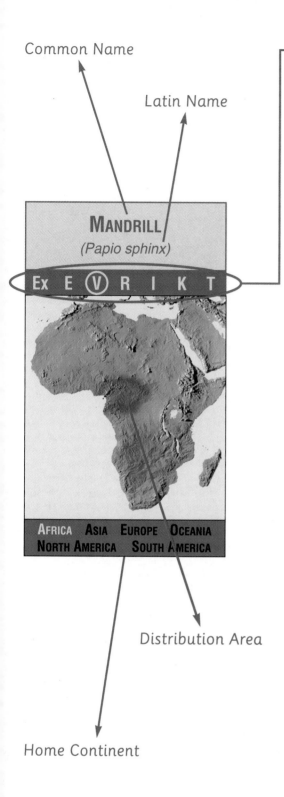

MANDRILL
(Papio sphinx)

Ex E Ⓥ R I K T

AFRICA ASIA EUROPE OCEANIA
NORTH AMERICA   SOUTH AMERICA

Distribution Area

Home Continent

CATEGORIES OF ENDANGERMENT

The categories of endangerment used in this encyclopedia are those set by the IUCN (International Union for Conservation of Nature and Natural Resources). The IUCN is an international organization responsible for compiling the *Red List of Threatened Animals*. The abbreviations used throughout this series are explained below.

(Ex) EXTINCT
Animals not seen in the wild during the past 50 years.

(E) ENDANGERED
Animals in danger of extinction and whose survival is unlikely if the factors that have put them in danger continue to affect them. Species whose numbers have decreased to a critical level or whose habitats have been drastically reduced are included in this category. Animals that may be extinct but that have been seen in the wild in the last 50 years also are considered "endangered."

(V) VULNERABLE
Animals that will be considered "endangered" in the future if the factors that currently threaten them continue. Also included in this category are animals whose populations have been reduced because of overexploitation, extensive destruction of habitat, or any other environmental disturbance; animals whose populations have been drastically reduced and whose survival is not guaranteed; and animals whose populations, although large, are threatened by dangerous conditions throughout the habitat.

(R) RARE
Animals with small populations that, although not currently considered "endangered" or "vulnerable," are at risk. These animals usually are found in limited territories or habitats, or are scattered over wide areas.

(I) INDETERMINATE
Species that belong in the "endangered," "vulnerable," or "rare" categories but about which not enough information is known to label them.

(K) INSUFFICIENTLY KNOWN
Animals believed to belong to one of the above categories, but about which reliable information is lacking.

(T) THREATENED
Species considered "endangered," "vulnerable," "rare," "indeterminate," or "insufficiently known" when not enough is known about them to place them in one specific category. This term also is used when the subspecies of a species belong in different categories.

BARBARY HYENA
(Hyaena hyaena barbara)

Ex (E) V R I K T

AFRICA ASIA EUROPE OCEANIA
NORTH AMERICA SOUTH AMERICA

DESCRIPTION
The Barbary Hyena looks like a large dog at first glance. Its bristly fur is a gray or light gray-brown color with dark brown or black stripes on the back and limbs. The striping is more obvious during the summer, when the fur is short. The fur is quite a lot longer in the winter. The hyena has a mane on its back, growing up to a foot long, which it can erect when it meets an enemy. The jaw is very solid, the ears are large, and the tail is long and thick. This hyena also has a well-developed sense of smell.

RELATED SPECIES
It is a member of the *Hyaena hyaena* species, which can be found in north, central, and east Africa and in southeast Asia. The Barbary Hyena is the northern subspecies.

SIZE
- Length: 3¼ to 4 feet
- Weight: 60 to 120 pounds
- Length of tail: about 1 foot

HABITAT
The Barbary Hyena lives in the mountainous areas and plateaus of North Africa. At one time widespread throughout this region, it is now confined to the Great Atlas Mountains, the Middle Atlas Mountains, the Taza Mountains, and the mountains of Urme. It also has been sighted on the plateaus between the border of Algeria and Tunisia.

DIET
The Barbary Hyena usually searches for food at dusk. Often called a "garbage man," it feeds on the carcasses of animals that are left by other predators. It also is not uncommon to see this animal near human settlements, where it takes advantage of food that is thrown away. Nevertheless, the Barbary Hyena's normal prey is small mammals, reptiles, birds, and insects. In addition, a large part of its diet is made up of fruit. The hyena's strong jaws allow it to grind up bones so that there is almost nothing left when it is finished eating.

Hunting has brought the Barbary Hyena to the brink of extinction.

1

THE YOUNG

The gestation period lasts about three months. Usually, two to four young are born, or sometimes five or six. The young are born blind and with their ears closed. They weigh about 1½ pounds at birth. After about eight days, the eyes open and the young animals are ready to start walking. Within a month, they are ready to feed from the prey that the mother brings. The young remain with the mother until about 5 months of age, when they are ready to live alone. They become sexually mature at 2 to 3 years of age.

INTERESTING FACTS

- The Barbary Hyena does not usually attack people and can be caught quite easily.

- It has become known as a coward.

- This animal walks on the tips of its toes rather than on the surface of its paws.

- The Barbary Hyena has lived to the age of 24 years in captivity.

ESTIMATED REMAINING POPULATION

An estimate dating back to 1977 reported that about 400 to 500 Barbary Hyenas remained in North Africa. Experts believe it is in serious danger of extinction.

REASONS FOR ENDANGERMENT

The Barbary Hyena has been actively hunted by humans because it is considered a danger to domestic animals and because natives fear it will pass the rabies epidemic on to the domestic stock. For the North African Tuareg, hyena meat also was considered a precious source of food. In addition, the Barbary Hyena's habitat has been significantly reduced, resulting in a decline in its numbers.

CONSERVATION MEASURES

The Barbary Hyena has been protected by law in Morocco since 1955. This animal also is protected by the 1969 African Convention, which prohibits its capture unless special authorization is granted. A few surviving populations live in some of North Africa's national parks and reserves.

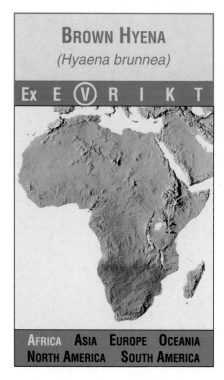

BROWN HYENA
(Hyaena brunnea)

Ex E (V) R I K T

AFRICA   ASIA   EUROPE   OCEANIA
NORTH AMERICA   SOUTH AMERICA

DESCRIPTION

The shaggy fur of the Brown Hyena sometimes is up to 8 inches long. The coloring of its coat is brown except on the lower parts, where it is lighter. It has a few stripes on the hind legs and a long, grayish mane down the middle of its back. The neck and shoulders are almost white. This animal has pointed ears and strong teeth.

SIZE

- Height at the withers: about 2 feet

- Length: about 3 to 3¼ feet

- Weight: 85 to 90 pounds

The Barbary Hyena usually searches for food at dusk.

▶ HABITAT

The arid savanna areas of the southern part of Africa are home to this animal. It can be found in the dry open plains and in dry tree-covered savannas. It spends most of the day in shelters dug out of the ground among the rocks. Its range includes South Africa (in the Kalahari National Park, the Kimberley District, and the eastern Cape District), southern Mozambique, southern Zimbabwe, Angola, Botswana, and Namibia.

▶ DIET

Like other hyenas, the Brown Hyena is the "garbage man" of the savanna's ecosystem. It usually eats the remains of animals that have been killed by other predators. It eats carcasses in a very unusual way. Each hyena takes a turn in tearing off a strip of meat and carrying it away to eat in private. At times, the hyena also eats small mammals, birds and their eggs, insects, and fruit. In coastal areas, it has been known to eat crabs and dead fish.

The Brown Hyena often eats the remains of animals killed by other predators.

▶ THE YOUNG

The male and female hyena do not stay together after mating. After a gestation period of about three months, the female gives birth to two or three offspring. On rare occasions, up to five may be born. The young are brought up in lairs for 15 days. After only three months they are able to eat meat, and within one year they become completely independent.

INTERESTING FACTS

- Although the Brown Hyena walks slowly, it can run faster than 30 miles per hour.

- Its life span hardly ever exceeds 12 to 13 years in the wild.

- A single hyena covers an average of 20 miles a night searching for food.

- This hyena is shy, and it is always ready to run away.

- It marks its territory with a white liquid that it secretes from its anal glands.

ESTIMATED REMAINING POPULATION

Unknown

REASONS FOR ENDANGERMENT

The continuous decrease in the Brown Hyena population is due mainly to slaughter carried out by settlers. The local people believe they must kill the Brown Hyena to protect their domestic animals.

CONSERVATION MEASURES

For now, this animal is fully protected only in the national parks and reserves in which it is found. It also is listed in Class B of the 1969 African Convention, which prohibits hunting of the animal without special authorization.

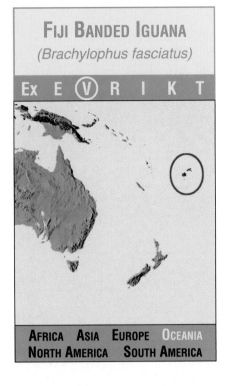

FIJI BANDED IGUANA
(Brachylophus fasciatus)

Ex E (V) R I K T

AFRICA ASIA EUROPE OCEANIA
NORTH AMERICA SOUTH AMERICA

DESCRIPTION

The coloring of the Fiji Banded Iguana is unusual, and it can change at different times during this animal's life. Normally this iguana displays two or three bright blue-green bands around its body. These bands stand out against the darker green background. The color contrast increases in the presence of an enemy. The crest along the iguana's back is not very high. The female looks very much like the male except for its slightly thinner limbs and a longer tail.

SIZE

- Length (including the tail): about 2⅓ feet

HABITAT

The favorite habitat of the Fiji Banded Iguana is the coastal and forest regions, often close to swamps. This animal inhabits the Fiji and Tonga islands.

DIET

It feeds on leaves, fruit, and a variety of insects.

BREEDING AND THE NEST

From January to March, the female enters the territory of the chosen male and mating begins. In May, she finds a bushy area near the beach, where she lays the eggs. The 1-inch eggs are laid in groups of three to six at a time. After a short time, the eggs absorb water from their surroundings and expand to about 1½ inches. The eggs are a whitish color with a brownish, oval-shaped spot that indicates the point at which the head of the unborn iguana will emerge.

THE YOUNG

Parental care seems to be well developed. Young Fiji Banded Iguanas have been observed following their parents about on trees.

INTERESTING FACTS

- The Fiji Banded Iguana's tail accounts for more than ⅔ of its total length.

- The iguana uses its tail for balance as it moves through its habitat.

- If an enemy approaches, the background color of the Fiji Banded Iguana turns very dark in about two to four minutes.

- It is very difficult to see this reptile among the trees in the forest.

- During the night, the iguana rests stretched out on tree branches or dangling from one branch by holding on with its front legs and using its tail as a counterbalance.

▶ ESTIMATED REMAINING POPULATION

Unknown

▶ REASONS FOR ENDANGERMENT

The introduction of the mongoose into this reptile's habitat has caused a severe decline in its population. In addition, humans clear the inhabited areas of trees and, frightened by the appearance of the iguana, kill it. This iguana also is captured and sold to merchants who export it to the United States and Europe, where it is sought after on the terrarium market.

▶ CONSERVATION MEASURES

Today, anyone found capturing, transporting, or keeping a Fiji Banded Iguana is issued a large fine.

The Fiji Banded Iguana's color darkens when an enemy is near.

ANEGADA GROUND IGUANA
(Cyclura pinguis)

Ex (E) V R I K T

AFRICA ASIA EUROPE OCEANIA
NORTH AMERICA SOUTH AMERICA

▶ DESCRIPTION

The Anegada Ground Iguana has a robust body supported by four limbs, each with five toes. Its mottled coloring serves as an effective camouflage in its habitat. The scales along the iguana's crest are clearly visible. The male has a large fold of skin at the neck which can be extended to enhance its appearance.

▶ HABITAT

The Anegada Ground Iguana prefers the lush tropical climate of the Virgin Islands. This animal lives among the palm, bamboo, ebony, and cedar trees, as well as among the magnolias and wild orchids that grow in the limestone areas of these islands.

▶ DIET

Its diet consists of a variety of plants.

▶ THE YOUNG

Between April and June, the female lays her eggs in a hole that is dug in the ground. After an incubation period of about three to four months, the young hatch. The young iguanas quickly disappear to escape predators or to seek safety in the undergrowth. The main predators of the young are some varieties of birds and nonpoisonous snakes.

▶ LAZY NATURE

The Anegada Ground Iguana is, by nature, a lazy creature. Those living on the island of Anegada can remain immobile for hours. In fact, almost 90% of their active life is spent in immobility. Even the males, during the mating season, remain inactive for more than 80% of the time.

▶ INTERESTING FACTS

- The Anegada Ground Iguana can reach an age of 40 years.

- This iguana probably owes its long life to its slow rate of metabolism.

- This species was first scientifically described in 1917.

▶ ESTIMATED REMAINING POPULATION

About 300 Anegada Ground Iguanas survive, and experts believe that number is on the decline.

▶ REASONS FOR ENDANGERMENT

The main reason for the decline in the Anegada Ground Iguana population is the destruction of its food source by domestic animals. Goats cause the greatest damage because they pull up entire plants, including the roots, which prevents regrowth.

▶ CONSERVATION MEASURES

The Anegada Ground Iguana has been protected by CITES (Convention on International Trade in Endangered Species) since 1973. This law has helped control the trade of the iguana and is enforced with severe penalties. In addition, part of the island of Anegada has been declared the British Virgin Islands National Park. All the plants and animals located in the park are protected and domestic animals are prohibited from this area. Additional studies must be undertaken before more protective measures can be adopted.

The Anegada Ground Iguana is active only about 10% of the time.

SAN SALVADOR GROUND IGUANA
(Cyclura rileyi)

Ex **E** **V** **R** (**I**) **K** **T**

AFRICA ASIA EUROPE OCEANIA
NORTH AMERICA SOUTH AMERICA

DESCRIPTION

The San Salvador Ground Iguana resembles other iguanas except for three differences. First, this iguana does not have widened prefrontal scales. Second, it has no single scales. Finally, it has a very noticeable dorsal crest that begins at the back of the skull and ends near the beginning of its tail.

RELATED SPECIES

The species is divided into two subspecies, *C.r. cristata* and *C.1 rileyi.*

HABITAT

The San Salvador Ground Iguana is distributed throughout the Bahamas archipelago. It prefers limestone terrain that is covered with the brush and vegetation found in arid regions.

LAZY NATURE

Under the cloudless skies of the Bahamas islands, this iguana easily regulates its body temperature and spends most of the day immobile. Its only activities are finding food, courting, mating, and raising territorial disputes during the mating season.

The female San Salvador Ground Iguana sometimes is killed for its eggs.

INTERESTING FACTS

- This so-called "little dragon" is not harmful to humans.

- Local inhabitants consider the eggs of this species a delicacy. The females' stomachs often are cut open to obtain eggs.

- Its only natural enemy is the wild pig, which was introduced to the islands by humans.

- This animal shares its habitat peacefully with many brightly colored fish and birds, including the flamingo.

ESTIMATED REMAINING POPULATION

Unknown

REASONS FOR ENDANGERMENT

Apart from hunting by the native population, who use the iguana for food, the main reason for this species' decline is the hunting carried out to supply the American and European markets. The treatment given this peaceful lizard as it is exported and sold is horrendous. In order not to ruin the skin, the iguana is often refrigerated live to prevent the rapid deterioration of the carcass. Even worse, those that are to be sold live are crowded into sacks or boxes with their limbs tied and mouths sewn shut to prevent them from injuring one another while they are being transported. In these conditions, without food or water, up to 90% of the captured specimens die before they reach their destination.

CONSERVATION MEASURES

The government of the Bahamas has passed protective laws for this iguana, but the laws have not yet been effective. This species also has been protected by CITES (Convention on International Trade in Endangered Species) since 1973. Veterinary controls at incoming and outgoing customs posts are not sufficient because only the few iguanas that have survived the initial journey are returned to their native surroundings. Further provisions and protective areas are needed in order to save the San Salvador Ground Iguana.

GALAPAGOS LAND IGUANA
(Conolophus subcristatus)

Ex E (V) R I K T

AFRICA ASIA EUROPE OCEANIA
NORTH AMERICA SOUTH AMERICA

DESCRIPTION

The Galapagos Land Iguana is a multicolored animal. Its head is lemon yellow. The coloring on its back varies from bright rusty red near the crest to a darker color on the sides of the body. The limbs are reddish yellow. The skin is completely covered by black dots. This lizard has a squat body with a high crest located only on the back of its neck.

SIZE

- Average weight (male): about 15 pounds

- Average weight (female): about 8 pounds

▶ HABITAT

This iguana is native to the Galapagos Islands. It prefers to live in the islands' dry regions, but sometimes inhabits damp, elevated areas.

▶ DIET

The Galapagos Land Iguana's diet consists of a variety of plants. Grubs and grasshoppers also are food sources for this animal, especially for young iguanas.

▶ BREEDING HABITS

This iguana is very territorial. In the weeks preceding coupling, there are many battles. Once the females arrive, they choose their mates and enter their territory. Many females may choose the same male, while other males may remain

The size of the Galapagos Land Iguana varies according to the amount of food available.

without a mate. They do not give up, however. The lonely male penetrates another's territory and a fight begins that can last hours, or even days. The female often leaves with the new male.

THE NEST

The female enters a volcano's crater and climbs down almost 3,000 feet inside. There she digs a hole in the ash and lava about 12 to 16 inches deep. In the hole, she lays from seven to 23 eggs and remains nearby to protect her nest. The eggs are incubated by the heat in the surrounding soil. The young are born in October. Few Galapagos Land Iguanas survive to adulthood because they are prey for snakes and hawks.

INTERESTING FACTS

• The size of this animal varies depending on the amount of food available.

• One study found one adult male to weigh as much as 26 pounds, while another adult male weighed as little as 11 pounds.

• This iguana has 23 to 24 teeth on each jaw.

• It is close to extinction on many of the Galapagos islands except Fernandina, which is the site of one of the world's most active volcanoes.

ESTIMATED REMAINING POPULATION

The number of existing Galapagos Land Iguanas is unknown, but experts say the species is in danger of extinction.

REASON FOR ENDANGERMENT

Wild cats, dogs, and pigs that have been introduced to the islands by humans ruthlessly hunt the Galapagos Land Iguana.

CONSERVATION MEASURES

The Galapagos Islands are now national parks and it is against the law to hunt or capture the Galapagos Land Iguana. In addition, this species is protected by CITES (Convention on International Trade in Endangered Species). Some thought is being given to the effects that the large numbers of tourists might have on the animals in this area. In addition, serious attempts are being made to control the population of wild cats, dogs, and pigs in this animal's habitat.

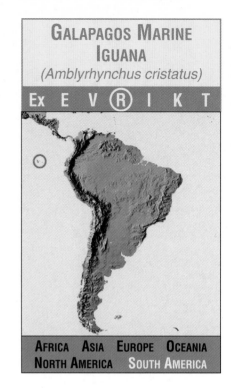

GALAPAGOS MARINE IGUANA
(Amblyrhynchus cristatus)

Ex E V (R) I K T

AFRICA ASIA EUROPE OCEANIA
NORTH AMERICA SOUTH AMERICA

DESCRIPTION

The Galapagos Marine Iguana's coloring changes with age. Adults have a grayish background color with dark spots. Its limbs have gray spots, and the under parts are yellowish brown. The crest consists of alternating yellow and black stripes. In the young, light gray spots are clearly evident on the black background of the head and flanks. This iguana has a strong, squat body with short, muscular limbs. Each limb has five webbed toes with curved claws. The head is short and wide with large, pointed shields. All of these traits give this peaceful animal a menacing appearance.

RELATED SPECIES

The *Amblyrhynchus cristatus* is divided into several subspecies.

Galapagos Marine Iguanas often gather in groups to keep their body temperatures warm.

SIZE

- Length (including tail): about 4½ feet

- Length of tail: about 2½ feet

HABITAT

This iguana is found on the Galapagos Islands, especially Fernandina Island. It must have a marine environment to survive. Its food, safety, and mobility depend on access to water.

DIET

The Galapagos Marine Iguana eats only algae. Its favorite algae is ulva, a variety with wide, pale green and red leaves. This iguana spends most of the day waiting at the water's edge for the waves and currents to carry piles of algae onto the rocks.

THE NEST

Egg laying depends on the availability of food, which changes with the seasons. Normally, this coincides with low tide, when food is easiest to obtain. Temperature also is an important factor. The nests are small holes that are carefully covered over to protect the eggs. The female deposits two or three eggs in the nest. She remains nearby to stand guard, compacting the ground and covering it with bits of debris from time to time.

THE YOUNG

The young hatch unaided. At birth, they weigh about 2½ ounces and are about 4 to 5 inches long. Most of the young do not reach adulthood. Some are swept away by waves that are too strong for their weak muscles to resist. Others are carried off by predators including the Barn Owl, the common Owl, certain species of snake, and, most dangerous of all, the Galapagos Hawk.

THE HEAP

It is very important for this iguana to conserve energy and to maintain its body temperature. For this reason, it has developed an unusual habit. In late afternoon, when the air grows cooler and the sky darkens, the iguanas gather on the beaches, often sheltered by rocky masses, and situate themselves in large heaps. All heads are turned toward the center of the heap and the tails are held outward. The adult males remain around the outside, while the females and the young usually are found toward the center and top of the pile. It is not certain whether this ritual is performed only to offset heat loss or whether it also may be done to protect the females and young from predators or even to aid in digestion. Whatever the reason, they break up the heap about three or four hours after sunrise.

INTERESTING FACTS

• The Galapagos Marine Iguana uses its tail to propel itself through water.

• It is a good swimmer in calm water and descends to considerable depths.

• The Galapagos Marine Iguana remains motionless for hours in the sun working to maintain a body temperature of 95 to 98.6°F.

• It is the only lizard to depend entirely on a marine environment.

ESTIMATED REMAINING POPULATION

Unknown

REASONS FOR ENDANGERMENT

Several factors have contributed to this iguana's endangerment. In addition to having limited success with reproduction, this animal is not able to defend itself well on land. As a result, it is threatened by wild dogs and cats that people have brought to the area. In addition, over the years, thousands of these creatures have been caught by people for food.

CONSERVATION MEASURES

Ecuador has declared the whole Galapagos peninsula a national park, forbidding the capture or removal of all native species. The Galapagos Marine Iguana also is protected by the CITES (Convention on International Trade in Endangered Species) treaty, and a program is under way to limit the number of wild dogs and cats on the islands. Only a few of these animals are alive in zoos. The unusual diet and social habits of this species make it difficult to breed in captivity.

The Galapagos Marine Iguana is the only lizard to depend on a marine environment.

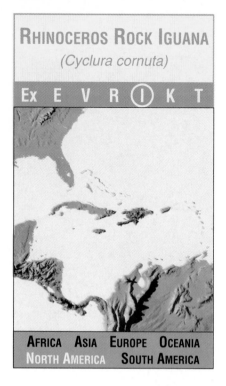

RHINOCEROS ROCK IGUANA
(Cyclura cornuta)

Ex **E V R** (I) **K T**

AFRICA ASIA EUROPE OCEANIA
NORTH AMERICA SOUTH AMERICA

▶ DESCRIPTION

The coloring of the Rhinoceros Rock Iguana is a drab shade of olive-gray that sometimes is crossed with darker stripes. This animal has a thick body that is covered with streamlined scales. A well-developed crest runs along its back. The Rhinoceros Rock Iguana can be distinguished from others of the same family by the horny knobs, usually two or three, that are found above the nose. The female Rhinoceros Rock Iguana is much smaller than the male.

▶ RELATED SPECIES

It is a member of the *Cyclura* family, typical island lizards that are divided into numerous species and subspecies.

▶ HABITAT

The very arid areas on the islands of Haiti and Mona are the preferred habitat of the Rhinoceros Rock Iguana. These areas include steppes that have many cacti and thorny bushes. The iguana is often found among grasses and thorny plants.

DIET

The Rhinoceros Rock Iguana is a vegetarian. It prefers the most tender parts of fibrous plants and the juicy flesh of cactus plants.

THE NEST

The pregnant female locates a nesting site where, in holes dug in the sand, she lays from eight to 24 eggs. This is a large number of eggs for this subspecies, but many of the young are lost to predators such as birds, snakes, other lizards, crabs, and wild pigs.

THE YOUNG

The newly hatched iguanas are fairly large. Each one measures about 3 to 4 inches in length. The larger size enables the young to leave the nest sooner in search of food.

INTERESTING FACTS

- During the winter, food sources are limited so the Rhinoceros Rock Iguana slows its metabolism to conserve energy.

- The horns of the male iguana are used for defense during territorial disputes.

- The eggs of this iguana are very large and can constitute a large percentage of the female's total body weight.

ESTIMATED REMAINING POPULATION

The number of existing Rhinoceros Rock Iguanas is not known, but experts say the species is in danger of extinction.

Male Rhinoceros Rock Iguanas use their horns to do battle.

REASONS FOR ENDANGERMENT

One of the greatest problems facing the Rhinoceros Rock Iguana is the lack of nesting sites on Mona Island, where less than 1% of the land is suitable for nesting. The females must migrate to find nesting sites and often have to share nests because of the limited space. As a result, when one nest is destroyed, many young are killed. Industrial and commercial development in the form of hotels and tourist attractions also have contributed to the decline in the Rhinoceros Rock Iguana population. Furthermore, the iguana's trusting nature in the presence of hunters has brought about a decrease in numbers and the risk of extinction.

CONSERVATION MEASURES

The Rhinoceros Rock Iguana is legally protected by Puerto Rican law and by the U.S. Endangered Species Act, which recognizes Mona Island as a "critical habitat" for the species. The capture and sale of this lizard is controlled by CITES (Convention on International Trade in Endangered Species), but there still is a need to protect this animal's habitat. Nesting sites must be fenced off or closed to the public, an educational program for tourists is needed, and serious efforts must be made to control the presence of wild goats, pigs, and cats.

JAGUAR
(Panthera onca)

Ex E Ⓥ R I K T

AFRICA ASIA EUROPE OCEANIA
NORTH AMERICA SOUTH AMERICA

DESCRIPTION

The coat of the Jaguar usually is a reddish, yellowish, or cinnamon color, tending to white on the belly. The fur is marked with dark spots and, for this reason, the Jaguar can be confused with other felines. However, the Jaguar's markings are distinct in that there are some small, dark spots in the center of the larger spots. These are completely absent in other members of the *Panthera* family. A type of black Jaguar, called "oncas" by the Brazilians, is not unusual. The Jaguar's head is massive and round, the muzzle short, and the ears small and rounded. The neck is strong and short with very few markings. The paws of the Jaguar have curved, grooved claws.

RELATED SPECIES

The Jaguar has given rise to several subspecies, each of which has adapted to a well-defined territory. They are the Arizona Jaguar, found in the southern part of the United States on the border the Mexico; the Yucatan Jaguar, found on the Yucatan Peninsula and in northern Guatemala; the Panama Jaguar, whose habitat ranges as far as Colombia; the Peruvian Jaguar, found in Ecuador and Bolivia; the Amazonian Jaguar, found in the Amazon; and the Parana Jaguar, today found in reduced areas in Brazil and Argentina.

SIZE

- Height at the shoulders: less than 3 feet

- Length of body: 4 to 6 feet

- Length of tail: 2½ to 3 feet

- Weight: 130 to 300 pounds

HABITAT

The Jaguar is a widespread and adaptable species. It lives in damp tropical forests and wooded areas, in savannas and grasslands where the grass is high enough to provide adequate cover. Although it prefers areas that have plenty of

The Jaguar can be confused with other felines because of the dark spots on its coat.

water, it also can be found in semidesert and rocky areas. Its territory extends from Arizona in the United States to Central and South America (see *Related Species*).

▶ DIET

The Jaguar usually hunts at dawn and sunset, and its normal prey consists of tapir, capybara, deer, monkeys, sloths, and small rodents.

Its favorite prey is the peccary, a wild pig that is similar to the boar.

▶ BREEDING AND THE YOUNG

After a gestation period of about 3½ months, the female Jaguar gives birth to two to four young. The cubs remain with the mother until they are 2 years old. It is believed that the Jaguar reproduces only every two years.

▶ HUNTING HABITS

The Jaguar's preferred hunting technique is the ambush, ending with a sudden leap onto the victim and a bite on the neck to sever the cervical vertebrate. It is an able swimmer and can catch fish with agility. It also catches caimans, which it manages to eat by boring through the reptile's armor with its strong claws.

TERRITORIES

The Jaguar is a very territorial animal. The size of each territory depends on the food supply, but usually ranges from 2 to 10 or more square miles. The Jaguars defend the borders of their territories from other males, but females often are permitted in other territories. This allows males and females to meet and mate during the reproductive season, the only period when Jaguars do not live alone.

INTERESTING FACTS

- Rare cases have been found of Jaguars measuring 10 feet in length and weighing up to 550 pounds.

- The Jaguar can climb trees and swim with ease, allowing it to live in areas that have frequent flooding.

- The female's coat is lighter than that of the male and has fewer spots.

- A type of albino Jaguar exists, but is very rare.

ESTIMATED REMAINING POPULATION

No estimates exist on the size of the various Jaguar populations, but from

A type of black Jaguar, called "oncas" by the Brazilians, is not unusual.

studies carried out and information obtained from various animal protection organizations, the species appears to be in a sharp decline.

REASONS FOR ENDANGERMENT

The large demand for Jaguar skins has caused a great reduction in this species' numbers. The market for this animal's skin, which is considered the most valuable of all feline skins, still flourishes. Some 20 years ago, a Jaguar skin was worth $80 to $130. Another factor contributing to this animal's decline is deforestation and the resulting reduction in its natural prey.

CONSERVATION MEASURES

Today, the Jaguar is largely confined to vast territories that belong to cattle breeders. Many of these areas have been turned into animal reserves. Although laws are in place to protect this species from hunting, the Jaguar still is killed for its skin.

DORIA'S TREE KANGAROO
(Dendrolagus dorianus)

Ex E Ⓥ R I K T

AFRICA   ASIA   EUROPE   OCEANIA
NORTH AMERICA   SOUTH AMERICA

DESCRIPTION

The coat of the Doria's Tree Kangaroo is mostly shades of brown. The back and shoulders are slightly darker brown, while the neck and paws have a silver coloring. The snout, eyes, and throat are blackish gray. The hairs of the coat are quite long, measuring about an inch. The tail has a mottled appearance. The digits of the front paws are armed with powerful claws.

RELATED SPECIES

This species is made up of three subspecies: *D.n. notatus*, *D.n. majrie*, and *D.n. dorianus*, all of New Guinea.

SIZE

- Length: about 2 feet

- Length of tail: about 1½ feet

▶ DIET
Leaves and bark make up the diet of the Doria's Tree Kangaroo.

▶ HABITAT
The tropical forests of New Guinea are home to the Doria's Tree Kangaroo. Although it can move around on the ground, this animal also can maneuver skillfully through the trees, where no predators can pursue it.

The thick coat of the Doria's Tree Kangaroo helps to protect it from the rainstorms of the tropical forest.

INTERESTING FACTS

- The Doria's Tree Kangaroo curls up and hides its head between its shoulders when it rains so that the water runs off easily.

- The hairs of its thick coat turn in the angle of the water so that rain is repelled.

- This animal's front paws have sharp claws for tearing leaves and bark from trees for food.

ESTIMATED REMAINING POPULATION

The number of existing Doria's Tree Kangaroos is unknown, but experts say the species is in danger of extinction.

REASONS FOR ENDANGERMENT

The Doria's Tree Kangaroo is considered in danger of extinction because of relentless hunting.

CONSERVATION MEASURES

Legislation must be created to ensure the survival of the Doria's Tree Kangaroo. The establishment of a protective area also is needed to save this species from extinction.

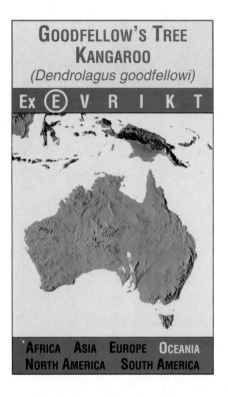

GOODFELLOW'S TREE KANGAROO
(Dendrolagus goodfellowi)

Ex E V R I K T

AFRICA ASIA EUROPE OCEANIA
NORTH AMERICA SOUTH AMERICA

DESCRIPTION

The Goodfellow's Tree Kangaroo has a tawny-colored coat. It is easily recognized by two yellow stripes that run along its back on either side of the spinal column. The same yellow color is found on the front and back paws and the underside, running from the throat to the tail. Like other kangaroos, this animal has the marsupial pouch in which the young develop after birth.

RELATED SPECIES

The *D.g. goodfellowi* species includes three subspecies: *D.g. goodfellowi*, *D.g. burgesi*, and *D.g. shawmayeri*, the most threatened subspecies.

HABITAT

The Goodfellow's Tree Kangaroo lives in the eastern part of New Guinea (Papua). It can be found in rocky, mountainous areas at altitudes of about 4,000 feet. Before European settlers came to New Guinea, this kangaroo lived at lower altitudes.

DIET

The Goodfellow's Tree Kangaroo is a herbivore. It eats a variety of leaves and plants. It passes most of its time in trees, and remains on the ground only briefly to search for food and water.

ADAPTATION

The Goodfellow's Tree Kangaroo has several structural traits that enable it to survive as an arboreal (tree-dwelling) animal. The lower surfaces of the paws have thick, well-developed pads that are covered with tough skin. These pads absorb the impact when the kangaroo makes long jumps. This animal has been seen leaping to the ground from a height of 60 feet. It also jumps from one branch to another for distances of up to 30 feet. It uses its tail to maintain balance while it moves about through the trees.

Left, the Goodfellow's Tree Kangaroo jumps skillfully among the trees.
Above, a young kangaroo develops in the marsupial pouch after birth.

INTERESTING FACTS

- Unlike most tree animals, the Goodfellow's Tree Kangaroo does not have a prehensile (grasping) tail.

- The fur on the head and neck of this animal are arranged so that rain will run off quickly to avoid excessive heat loss.

- Unlike other kangaroos, the front and back limbs of the Goodfellow's Tree Kangaroo are almost the same length.

ESTIMATED REMAINING POPULATION

The number of existing Goodfellow's Tree Kangaroos is unknown, but experts say the species is in danger of extinction.

REASONS FOR ENDANGERMENT

When on the ground, this kangaroo is vulnerable and easily captured by the aborigines who eat its meat. Also a problem is the loss of habitat that this animal has suffered due to human pressures.

CONSERVATION MEASURES

Currently, no measures are in place to protect the Goodfellow's Tree Kangaroo.

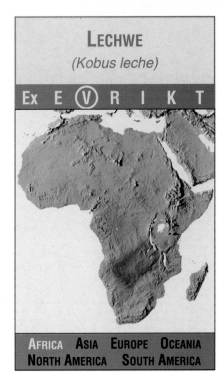

LECHWE
(Kobus leche)

Ex E (V) R I K T

AFRICA ASIA EUROPE OCEANIA
NORTH AMERICA SOUTH AMERICA

DESCRIPTION

Scientists have identified three subspecies of Lechwe, which differ in the color of the coat and geographical distribution. The coloring varies from chestnut brown to darker, almost black, colors. The underbelly on all three subspecies is pale, and the legs are dark in front with a black stripe and a white spot just above each hoof. The horns, present only in the male Lechwe, are rather thin and take the shape of a lyre.

RELATED SPECIES

The Lechwe is a species of antelope. The three subspecies are the Red Lechwe, the Kafue Lechwe, and the Black Lechwe.

SIZE

- Height at the withers: 3 to 3½ feet

- Weight (average male): about 180 pounds

- Weight (average female): about 140 pounds

- Length of horns: 2⅓ to 3 feet

HABITAT

The humid, marshy areas of central-southern Africa are home to the Lechwe.

DIET

The Lechwe is a herbivore. This animal perfers the tender, newly grown grass that is found in the regions where the evaporation of water in the marshes causes sprouts and shoots to grow rapidly.

TERRITORIES

During the mating season, from November to early January, the male Lechwes gather in a somewhat restricted area and defend their own personal territories. They do not, however, fight against one another. This particular kind of territorialism can be found in only two species of mammals, the Lechwe and the Uganda Kob. These small territories do not change in the years that follow. Females in heat enter the small territories of the various males, forming numerous harems.

▶ INTERESTING FACTS

- The Lechwe has very long, sharp hooves that help it adapt to its damp environment.

- It migrates every year, according to the progress of the dry season.

- There may be as many as 1,000 members in a herd of Lechwe.

▶ ESTIMATED REMAINING POPULATION

Remaining populations for each subspecies are as follows:

- A few populations of Red Lechwe exist, for a total of about 35,000 animals.

The Lechwe is in danger of extinction because of hunting and because of the destruction of its natural habitat.

- A single population of Black Lechwe exists, consisting of fewer than 40,000 specimens.

- One population of Kafue Lechwe exists in Zambia, consisting of about 25,000 animals.

▶ REASONS FOR ENDANGERMENT

The two main causes for the decrease in the Lechwe population are hunting and the exploitation of its natural environment by humans. This animal is hunted because people enjoy the taste of its meat and value the Lechwe horns as hunting trophies. Further, the marshy areas where these antelopes live have undergone fast and drastic changes. Land reclamation, dikes, and river dams developed to improve irrigation have drastically altered the natural features of the Lechwe's land.

▶ CONSERVATION MEASURES

There are many natural reserves and national parks where the Lechwe roam. These areas provide protection for the Lechwe as well as for a variety of other animals. The Black and Kafue Lechwes also are protected by laws in various countries that have forbidden hunting. The Red Lechwe is not protected because laws in its favor have not been respected. Finally, attempts have been made to breed the Lechwe in captivity.

LEOPARD
(Panthera pardus)

Ex E (V) R I K T

AFRICA   ASIA   EUROPE   OCEANIA
NORTH AMERICA   SOUTH AMERICA

▶ DESCRIPTION

The African Leopard is an elegant and slender feline. Its coat usually is cinnamon, ocher, or yellowish in color, tending toward lighter shades on the flanks. The characteristic spots are rosette shaped. The size and spacing of these markings varies. The spots on the flanks and legs tend to be bigger and join together. The spots on the head are smaller and more numerous. The Leopard's head is fairly large and round in shape. This feline's greenish eyes and long white whiskers are striking.

▶ RELATED SPECIES

Various subspecies of the African Leopard exist, such as the North African Leopard, the Congo Leopard, the Eritrean Leopard, and the South African Leopard. The

Leopard is recognized as the most widespread feline when including both the African and Asian populations.

▶ SIZE

The Leopard is strong for its size. The measurements listed below represent the range of sizes for the various subspecies of adult male Leopards.

- Length: 3 to 5 feet

- Weight: 130 to 200 pounds

- Length of tail: 2 to 3 feet

▶ HABITAT

The African Leopard's environment is extremely varied. It can be found almost everywhere except in the middle of the Sahara Desert. In fact, it has been found living in the Kalahari Desert as well as in mountainous areas at altitudes of nearly 10,000 feet. It has even been sighted at altitudes as high as 15,000 feet. Nevertheless, the Leopard's favorite habitats are forests and plains where trees and plant growth are abundant. These areas provide the Leopard with a variety of prey and with good cover.

The Leopard's silence when searching for prey makes it an excellent hunter.

DIET

Baboons, impalas, gazelles, kudus, and small giraffes are the favorite prey of the Leopard. Nevertheless, it will eat a wide variety of foods. It also feeds on birds, snakes, moles, other small mammals, and even fruit. This adaptability to various foods has aided the Leopard in its survival.

The Leopard often takes its prey into trees so that other predators cannot snatch it.

FANCY FOOTWORK

The Leopard is one of the most silent animals in existence. It has a unique walk, almost tiptoeing. Its ability to place the back paws exactly where the forepaws were enables it to move without making noise. This has been confirmed by hunters and researchers who have had Leopards appear before them seemingly out of nowhere. This also makes the Leopard an excellent hunter.

HUNTING HABITS

The Leopard captures its prey by ambush or by using tricks to attract its attention. Unlike other cats, it does not leave its prey behind after it has eaten. It takes the remains to the top of a tree so that other predators, such as Jackals and Hyenas, cannot take it. The Leopard returns several times until it has eaten its fill. Until recently, scientists thought this animal hunted at night, but they discovered that the Leopard adopted this habit

The African Leopard is threatened because its habitat is shrinking. On the following pages, the Leopard's coat blends in with its habitat.

in response to its being hunted by people during the day.

▶ BREEDING AND THE YOUNG

In tropical regions where there is no drastic change in seasons, there is no precise mating time. After a gestation period of about three months, the female leopard gives birth to two to four cubs. The couple remains together after the birth of the young, sharing the parental responsibilities. The male provides the food for the whole family. The cubs grow quickly. By the time they are 5 months old, they are almost as large as their parents. The cubs remain with their parents until the next reproductive season.

INTERESTING FACTS

• The dark spots among the light areas on the Leopard's coat help to camouflage the animal in its environment.

• Respect and fear of the Leopard have led to a variety of beliefs and superstitions about it.

• The Leopard adapts very well to new environments and has survived even in inhospitable zones.

ESTIMATED REMAINING POPULATION

Exact numerical estimates are not known; however, Leopard populations seem to have remained stable. Although populations are diminishing in some zones, they are increasing in other areas where the Leopard is protected or not disturbed. In Zambia alone, there are thought to be nearly 20,000 Leopards remaining.

REASONS FOR ENDANGERMENT

Various factors threaten the Leopard. Its natural habitat is shrinking as herds of domestic cattle increase and new crops are harvested. Increased numbers of domestic cattle have stolen land from wild grazers. This has resulted in fewer wild ungulates and therefore less prey for the Leopard. This prompts the Leopard to attack domestic animals. Because of this, people consider the Leopard to be dangerous, and they use chemicals to kill it. This form of killing is the most serious threat to the Leopard. The slaughter of this feline to supply skins for the fur trade has added to the problem.

CONSERVATION MEASURES

Because the Leopard has the ability to adapt to changes in its natural environment, it can survive in areas that people do not want to inhabit. This is the case of a habitat called Miombo in central Africa, a savanna environment that is now considered a natural reserve. The species has been protected by CITES (Convention on International Trade in Endangered Species) since 1973. Local laws also have been established, with varying levels of effectiveness.

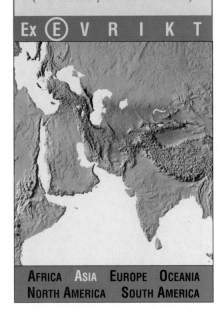

ANATOLIAN LEOPARD
(Panthera pardus tulliana)

Ex Ⓔ V R I K T

AFRICA ASIA EUROPE OCEANIA
NORTH AMERICA SOUTH AMERICA

DESCRIPTION

The Anatolian Leopard's coat is usually a vivid brown with shadings to gray. It has the typical rosette-shaped spots that are large with clearly marked edges. Its fur is short and silky.

RELATED SPECIES

The Anatolian Leopard is similar to the Leopard of the Caucasis (*P.p. ciscaucasica*) except that it is larger and has lower cheekbones and a broader forehead.

SIZE

• Length: 4½ to 6 feet

• Length of tail: 3½ to 4 feet

The Anatolian Leopard prefers conifer and broadleaf woods.

HABITAT

This feline prefers a habitat of conifer and broadleaf woods, but does not avoid bushy areas and open spaces. In the past, the Anatolian Leopard was numerous in the areas between Turkey, Iran, and Turkestan, ranging as far as Syria, Lebanon, and Israel. Today, a few specimens may survive in Turkey's national park at Kusadasi and in Iran and Afghanistan.

INTERESTING FACTS

• The Anatolian Leopard was described by Valenciennes in 1856.

• The Anatolian Leopard also is known as the leopard of the Transcaucasian snows.

ESTIMATED REMAINING POPULATION

No data exists on the size of the Anatolian Leopard population today. A census taken in Turkey in 1975 found only 15 to 23 animals remaining. Only five to eight specimens remained in Turkestan in 1976.

CLOUDED LEOPARD
(Neofelis nebulosa)

Ex E (V) R I K T

AFRICA ASIA EUROPE OCEANIA
NORTH AMERICA SOUTH AMERICA

▶ DESCRIPTION

As its name suggests, the soft, thick, woolly coat of the Clouded Leopard has markings that resemble clouds. The coat is ash gray or yellowish gray in color, becoming lighter on the belly. The cloudlike marks take the form of large rosettes, darker than the background color, and the borders are invariably black. The throat, belly, and paws are decorated with small, dark spots. The spots on the back form long stripes that extend to the neck and ears. The tail also has lines that form dark rings. The muzzle of the Clouded Leopard is typically feline, marked by yellowish eyes with slit-shaped pupils.

▶ RELATED SPECIES

Although known as a leopard by its common name, this species does not belong to the *Panthera* genus, but to the *Neofelis*. It is considered a kind of link between the two groups because it has characteristics that are common to both.

▶ SIZE

• Length: about 3¼ feet

• Weight: 35 to 50 pounds

• Length of tail: 2 to 3 feet

▶ HABITAT

The favorite habitat of the Clouded Leopard is forests with thick undergrowth. However, this animal also can be found in damp, marshy areas and has been sighted at altitudes as high as 6,500 feet. The distribution area of all the subspecies extends from northern India to Nepal and Bhutan and up to southern China. It also is found in Burma, Thailand, Taiwan, Borneo, Sumatra, and the Indonesian and Malay peninsulas.

▶ DIET

In trees, the Clouded Leopard captures monkeys, squirrels, and birds. It also can capture birds in flight. This feline catches larger prey, including boar, deer, and goats, by leaping down on them from tree branches. Before eating, it scrapes off any fur or feathers from its prey by using its rough tongue. It then tears off small mouthfuls by grasping the meat in its teeth and raising its head in sudden, jerky movements.

▶ BREEDING AND THE YOUNG

The female Clouded Leopard uses a tree cavity for a den. After a gestation period of about three months, it gives birth to two to four young. The cubs remain protected in the den for the first three weeks of life until their eyes are perfectly functioning. At this time, the mother begins to wean and train the cubs, preparing them for life in the trees.

▶ AGILITY

The Clouded Leopard is agile and slender, which allows it to maneuver easily through the trees. This feline can move along the branches with its back turned toward the ground, and can leap from one branch to another, keeping its grip with just one of its back legs. This leopard also can climb down tree trunks very rapidly, always keeping its head turned toward the ground.

The Clouded Leopard is hunted for its valuable coat, despite legislation prohibiting the trade of its skins.

The Clouded Leopard can capture deer and other large prey by leaping down on them from tree branches.

ESTIMATED REMAINING POPULATION

Accurate population figures are not available; however, the Clouded Leopard is believed to be extinct or nearing extinction in some of its territories.

REASONS FOR ENDANGERMENT

The main cause for the decline in the Clouded Leopard population is the high value placed on its skin. Especially in the 1960s and 1970s, this animal's attractive skin was considered quite fashionable. Deforestation undertaken to increase agricultural areas also has contributed to the decline of this species, whose very existence depends on a thickly wooded habitat. According to recent estimates, the forests in Thailand, which once covered more than 80% of the entire territory, now occupy only about 20%.

CONSERVATION MEASURES

The Clouded Leopard is legally protected in China, Thailand, and India. Even after the 1973 Washington International Convention, however, trade in animal skins continued illegally. Fortunately, this animal has reproduced successfully in captivity. Since the 1970s, more than 47 Clouded Leopards have been raised in captivity.

INTERESTING FACTS

• In Borneo, this animal is known as *hariman-dahan*, which means "tree tiger."

• In the 1970s, a Clouded Leopard skin was worth $150.

• During the daytime, the Clouded Leopard remains in its resting place among the trees.

KOREAN LEOPARD
(Panthera pardus orientalis)

Ex (E) V R I K T

AFRICA ASIA EUROPE OCEANIA
NORTH AMERICA SOUTH AMERICA

▶ DESCRIPTION

The fur of the Korean Leopard is golden and very shiny. Roundish spots with black borders cover its entire body and form the typical rosette design seen in leopards. The center of each spot is darker than the rest of the golden coat. This particular leopard has both a winter coat and a summer coat. The winter version is thicker and lighter in color than the summer coat. The front legs are shorter than the muscular hind legs. The Korean Leopard's head is longer and not as round as other felines.

▶ RELATED SPECIES

This leopard often is confused with the Snow Leopard because its coat is similar.

▶ SIZE

- Height at the shoulders: 2 to 2½ feet

- Weight: 60 to 80 pounds

- Length of body: 3½ to 4½ feet

- Length of tail: 2½ to 3 feet

▶ HABITAT

The Korean Leopard lives in the innermost parts of forests where the wooded areas alternate with rocky spurs, steep slopes, and plains. Here vegetation is formed of low bushes and scrub. In the western part of the former Soviet Union, its territories can be found particularly in hilly areas, while farther south in Manchuria and Korea, it can be found at altitudes of 3,500 to 5,000 feet.

Reservations have been created to protect the Korean Leopard.

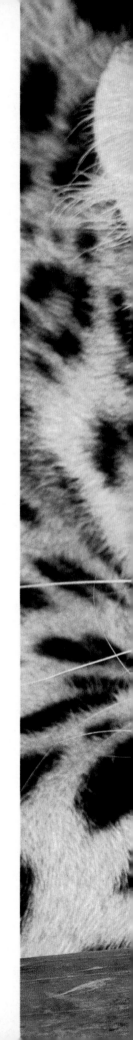

DIET

In addition to deer, the Korean Leopard's diet includes rodents, birds, foxes, and wolves. When necessary, this leopard also attacks domestic animals.

BREEDING AND THE YOUNG

A solitary animal, the Korean Leopard forms couples only during the mating season, which lasts from January to February. When it is time for the young to be born, the female Korean Leopard chooses the thickest, most inaccessible part of the forest. After a three-month gestation period, she gives birth to two to five young. The cubs remain with the mother until the next reproductive season.

HUNTING HABITS

This animal hunts primarily at dawn or sunset. It may attack its prey directly or use the ambush technique. It is able to climb rocks and trees with ease and to leap long distances. These abilities aid the Korean Leopard during the hunt.

INTERESTING FACTS

• When it was more abundant, the Korean Leopard was known in China by the name *initsyan-bao*, which means "the leopard whose spots are similar to silver coins."

• It is the northernmost Asiatic leopard.

• Specimens measuring nearly 8 feet in length have been captured.

ESTIMATED REMAINING POPULATION

The Korean Leopard already has been deemed extinct in many of its former territories. These include the Siberian provinces of Amur, extending as far as the northern regions of Korea and Manchuria, and China, where it became extinct in 1967. This species is believed to be near extinction in South Korea.

REASONS FOR ENDANGERMENT

Deforestation has caused the decline in the Korean Leopard population. This loss of habitat has led to a reduction in available prey for the leopard. Also contributing to its endangerment is extensive hunting for its beautiful skin.

CONSERVATION MEASURES

This leopard is legally protected in Korea, where steps are being taken to turn all areas that are important to its survival into national parks. In the former Soviet Union, the reservations of Sudzukhin and Sikhote Alin have been created to protect this animal.

The Korean Leopard is believed to be extinct in several of its former territories.

SNOW LEOPARD
(Panthera uncia)

Ex (E) V R I K T

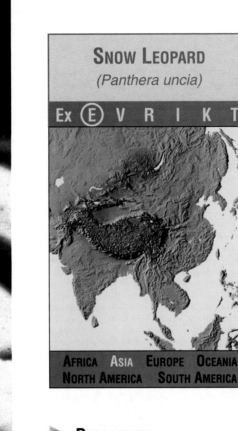

AFRICA **ASIA** EUROPE OCEANIA
NORTH AMERICA SOUTH AMERICA

▶ DESCRIPTION

The Snow Leopard, also called an irbis, is a large animal with yellowish fur patterned with black spots and small rings. Its head is rounded and its legs are agile and strong with large, padded feet and sharp claws. Its tail is more than half the length of its body.

▶ SIZE

• Length: 4 to 4½ feet

• Length of tail: 2½ to 3¼ feet

• Weight: 50 to 90 pounds

The Snow Leopard prefers rocky areas with several gorges in which to ambush prey.

▶ HABITAT

The Snow Leopard is well named because it lives in high, mountainous areas where there always is snow on the ground. Its favorite habitat is rocky areas rich in gorges and ravines where it uses its great jumping abilities to ambush its prey, surprising its victim by descending upon it. Once widely distributed throughout the mountains of Asia, the Snow Leopard can still be found in Nepal, Afghanistan, India, and Russia.

▶ DIET

The Snow Leopard's favorite prey are the wild goat and the Himalayan thar, in addition to ibex, deer, and boar. It also hunts domestic animals such as cattle if wild prey is scarce.

▶ BREEDING AND THE YOUNG

During the mating season, which usually is between January and March, the Snow Leopard forms fixed couples. After a pregnancy period of about 3 months, the female gives birth to two to five young. During the first six weeks, the cubs are totally dependent on the mother. Shortly afterward, however, the young are able to walk on rocky terrain and follow their mother. At 9 months of age, they are strong enough to kill large prey by themselves.

JUMPING ABILITY

The Snow Leopard is an exceptional jumper. Its strong legs enable it to take leaps of up to 50 feet. Its large paws allow it to easily walk on difficult and broken ground, without falling into the snow.

FUR

The animal's thick and woolly fur, which can be almost 3 inches long on the belly, protects it from cold winter weather. The coat is decorated with rosette-shaped markings, which are larger on the back and smaller and closer together on the flanks. This animal's light yellow to white coloring is more pronounced during the winter, and it tends toward gray during the summer.

TERRITORIES

The Snow Leopard is a territorial animal. It marks the borders of its territory with urine or by grooving marks on tree trunks with its claws. The hunting zones of individual leopards often overlap.

INTERESTING FACTS

- The Snow Leopard is a rare and solitary animal.

- This leopard is seldom seen by humans.

- It has been found as high as 20,000 feet above sea level during the summer.

- This animal is capable of withstanding a very cold climate.

- Snow Leopard skins recently were found on the black market priced at $60,000.

- In one case, a young 55-pound male Snow Leopard was recorded as having stalked and killed a wild male goat weighing about 132 pounds.

The Snow Leopard's coat is grayer in the summer and light yellow in the winter.

ESTIMATED REMAINING POPULATION

Experts believe that about 5,000 or fewer Snow Leopards survive worldwide.

REASONS FOR ENDANGERMENT

Hunters have killed the Snow Leopard for its beautiful and very valuable fur. Hunting is illegal in most of the territories where it lives; however, the skins of the leopard continue to appear in markets. The Snow Leopard also is killed by herders, who consider it a threat to their herds of cattle.

CONSERVATION MEASURES

The populations of the Snow Leopard are on a sharp decline throughout central Asia, but some preventative measures have been taken. In 1973, six parks and reserves were created in Nepal to protect this animal. One sanctuary was created in India, and several reserves have been created in Russia to help prevent the Snow Leopard from becoming extinct.

ASIATIC LION
(Panthera leo persica)

Ex (E) V R I K T

AFRICA ASIA EUROPE OCEANIA
NORTH AMERICA SOUTH AMERICA

DESCRIPTION

The Asiatic Lion is a large, tawny-colored animal with a massive, square-shaped body and a long tail. Its legs are strong and straight, ending in strong paws that have retractable, crescent-shaped claws. Its large head has a round muzzle and a mouth full of long, powerful teeth. This feline has very big, round, yellow eyes. The male has a long, thick mane.

RELATED SPECIES

It is related to the African Lion, which also belongs to the *Panthera leo* genus.

SIZE

• Length: 5½ to 6 feet

• Length of tail: 3 to 3½ feet

• Weight: up to 550 pounds

THE ROAR

Because of an elastic ligament in the thyroid, which forms part of the animal's neck, the lion is able to roar. It is the only feline in existence that can make roaring sounds.

THE MANE

The male Asiatic Lion has a thick mane, which is shorter and lighter-colored than that of the African Lion. The Asiatic species also has more fur and a longer tuft on the end of its tail.

HABITAT

This lion's preferred habitat is the great grasslands or tropical savannas dotted with trees. In ancient times, it was distributed throughout Greece, Syria, Palestine, Mesopotamia, Iran, and India. Today, the only place in the world where the Asiatic Lion can be found in the wild is the Gir Forest in India, which is now recognized as a national park and lion sanctuary.

DIET

The lion's main prey is the nilgaus, the porcine deer, the dappled deer, and the boar. If necessary, the lion also attacks domestic cattle. Its teeth are well developed for easily tearing up prey. The lion's four canine teeth are particularly large.

THE PRIDE

The lion lives in groups called prides, which can be made up of as many as 30 individuals. The male is dominant, but the female does most of the hunting for the pride.

BREEDING AND THE YOUNG

The peak mating period is October and November, though mating can occur at any time of the year. The female's pregnancy lasts 110 to 115 days. Two to five cubs are born at a time. Compared to the young of the African Lion, Asiatic Lion cubs have fewer markings, making the coat a more uniform color.

INTERESTING FACTS

• The lion is known as a symbol of power and courage.

• Several cities, including Venice, Italy, have adopted the lion as an emblem.

• A legendary animal, the lion appeared in prehistoric cave paintings and often is mentioned in the Bible.

• It has a horny stinger on its tail.

• The lion's sense of smell is extremely developed, and its sight and hearing also are acute.

The lion is the only feline that can make roaring sounds.

ESTIMATED REMAINING POPULATION

The lion population in Gir National Park seems to have stabilized at approximately 200 specimens.

REASONS FOR ENDANGERMENT

For some time, the lion was hunted by humans for sport. After humans decided to protect it and banned its being hunted, goats, sheep, and cows then began to threaten its existence. After

deforestation, nomads began to bring their herds into the lion's park to graze. The large influx of domestic animals that invaded the lion's territory had a disastrous effect on the ecosystem. This was seen at first in a reduction of wild herbivores, which are the lion's natural prey. The lion, therefore, was forced to hunt the domestic animals to satisfy its needs. This prompted the nomads to poison the lion. The park subsequently was closed to outsiders.

▶ **CONSERVATION MEASURES**
Gir National Park, home to the Asiatic Lion, is known as one of the best managed parks and reserves in India. There the lion population presently remains stable.

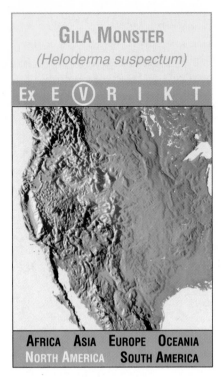

GILA MONSTER
(Heloderma suspectum)

Ex E Ⓥ R I K T

AFRICA ASIA EUROPE OCEANIA
NORTH AMERICA SOUTH AMERICA

DESCRIPTION
The Gila Monster is a large lizard with a poisonous bite. It has a large head, short legs, and a long, thick body and tail. Its skin is covered with beadlike scales, which generally are orange, salmon pink, black, and brown in color. The Gila Monster's limbs have five digits with sharp nails.

RELATED SPECIES
The Gila Monster is related to the Beaded Lizard, which is the only other lizard with a poisonous bite.

SIZE
• Length of trunk: about 1 to 1⅓ feet

• Length of tail: about 6 inches

HABITAT
The Gila Monster can be found in the deserts of the southwest United States and northwest Mexico. This lizard especially likes arid and semiarid regions on the lower slopes of mountains, wherever there is a water course.

DIET
A slow-moving hunter, the Gila Monster raids the nests of birds and other reptiles, searching for either eggs or young animals. It also feeds on small rodents.

BREEDING AND THE YOUNG
The Gila Monster reproduces only once every two years. During the mating season, the female digs a hole 3 to 5 inches deep in moist sand, near clumps of bushes shaded from the sun. In this hole, she lays between four and seven thick-shelled eggs measuring about 1½ to 3 inches in length. The hole is covered with sand. After approximately one month, the eggs hatch. The young lizards are about 4 inches in length and are capable of leaving the nest on their own shortly after birth.

THE SCALES
The scales of this lizard are wide and flat on the head, becoming more rounded on the back and the limbs. Generally, the head, body, and legs are marbled in various manners with stripes and patches of orange, salmon pink, black, and brown. The chin, neck, nose, and sides of the head are dark and dotted. The tail has barred rings.

POISONOUS BITE
The Gila Monster has poisonous saliva. Its large

The Gila Monster has a poison gland located behind its chin.

poison glands, located just behind the chin, release poison into the Gila Monster's mouth when it grips its prey. In order for the poison to sink in, the lizard must hold on tightly to its victim for at least a few minutes.

SURVIVAL TECHNIQUES

The Gila Monster overcomes the necessity for water by spending the dry months buried underground in a state of rest, or estivation, coming out only during the rainy season. The Gila Monster survives long periods of fasting by using the reserves of fat that accumulate in its tail.

INTERESTING FACTS

- The Gila Monster is basically a timid and solitary animal.

- It is extremely slow-moving and clumsy in its walk.

- It is one of only two poisonous lizards in the world today.

- No two Gila Monsters have the same coloring.

- Its thick tail acts as a food reservoir.

- If irritated, it will attack humans. This lizard's bite has been fatal to humans in only eight instances.

- The first known fossil remains of this lizard date back 30 to 40 million years and were found in Colorado.

ESTIMATED REMAINING POPULATION

The number of existing Gila Monsters is not known, but experts say the species is vulnerable.

REASONS FOR ENDANGERMENT

The Gila Monster has suffered from a loss of habitat due to farming, which has intensified since a system of irrigation was developed. Also contributing to this habitat loss is the grazing of domestic animals. Because the Gila Monster is such a peculiar animal, it also is highly prized on the live market. Therefore, many specimens are captured each year and shipped abroad to be sold.

CONSERVATION MEASURES

The Gila Monster does not reproduce well, or at all, in captivity. Therefore, the population in the wild must be protected. Tough laws have been created in Arizona, Utah, and Nevada to stop the illegal capturing and sale of the Gila Monster. This animal also is protected by the CITES (Convention on International Trade in Endangered Species) treaty.

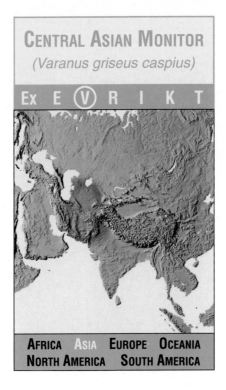

CENTRAL ASIAN MONITOR
(Varanus griseus caspius)

Ex E (V) R I K T

AFRICA ASIA EUROPE OCEANIA
NORTH AMERICA SOUTH AMERICA

DESCRIPTION

The Central Asian Monitor, also known as the Desert or Sand Monitor, is a large, aggressive lizard with a wide head and very powerful jaws. It has a thick body and a long tail with a rounded end. Its skin is covered with scales of a yellowish gray color, decorated with horizontal brown stripes. Its belly is yellow or beige.

RELATED SPECIES

The Central Asian Monitor is a member of the lizard family.

HABITAT

This lizard lives in central Asia in desertlike habitats or steppes, always in rocky areas near water. At one time, the monitor was widespread throughout northern Africa and Southeast Asia — more precisely, in Arabia, Pakistan, Iran, Afghanistan, Palestine, and the former Soviet Union.

RESPONSE TO DANGER

When disturbed, the Central Asian Monitor will give its enemy a brief warning with a series of distinctive body movements. Then it will raise itself several feet from the ground with its tail and attack its victim with its powerful jaws. The Central Asian Monitor has been known to attack camels, horses, and humans.

The Central Asian Monitor is an agressive lizard that has been known to attack horses, camels, and humans.

▶ INTERESTING FACTS

- The monitor has slim nostrils similar to cracks.

- Its tongue has two horny points.

- The Central Asian Monitor can be domesticated if it is trained at a young age.

▶ ESTIMATED REMAINING POPULATION

The number of existing Central Asian Monitors is unknown, but experts say the species is in danger of becoming extinct.

▶ REASONS FOR ENDANGERMENT

The Central Asian Monitor is endangered due to loss of habitat and indiscriminate capturing. Snake charmers file the lizards' teeth down and, after imprisoning them in leather bags with no food or water, sell them to unsuspecting tourists as docile pets.

▶ CONSERVATION MEASURES

This lizard is protected by the CITES (Convention on International Trade in Endangered Species) treaty. The Central Asian Monitor also is protected by law in Russia and in the nature reserves of Repetek, Bandkhys, and Tigrovaya.

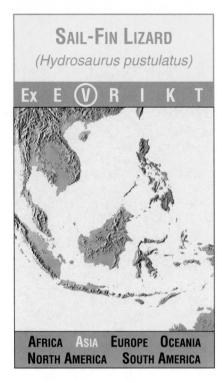

SAIL-FIN LIZARD
(*Hydrosaurus pustulatus*)

Ex E (V) R I K T

AFRICA ASIA EUROPE OCEANIA
NORTH AMERICA SOUTH AMERICA

DESCRIPTION

The Sail-fin Lizard derives its name from the sail-shaped crest of skin along the tail of the male. The male lizard is a brilliant green-brown color with a second smaller crest on its back. The female is less colorful and has no crests. Both have flat, muscular bodies that enable them to move easily through the water. As a member of the *Hydrosaurus* genus, it is well adapted to an aquatic environment.

RELATED SPECIES

It is related to the *Basiliscus* of South America.

SIZE

• Length: about 3 feet

HABITAT

The Sail-fin Lizard lives in tropical forests along the rivers and waterways of the Philippine Island and several of its surrounding islands. This archipelago is volcanic in origin and contains some of the lushest vegetation of any habitat on earth.

DIET

This small reptile enjoys a varied diet that includes fruits, leaves, centipedes, and insects.

BREEDING AND THE YOUNG

The female lays four to six eggs in a little hole dug in the vegetation. She then covers the hole with soil using her head and hind legs. The newborns are very timid and remain hidden as much as possible to avoid predators. They reach maturity at about 1½ years of age. The young female tends to remain in its area of birth, while the male goes in search of territory away from other male competitors.

MOVEMENT IN WATER

Because of its large, fleshy toes, the Sail-fin Lizard can hoist itself up and run for short distances along the surface of the water. It swims by making undulating, or side to side, movements.

THE CREST

The large crest of skin located on the male Sail-fin Lizard's tail is supported by long, bony projections. This crest can be as tall as 2½ inches and helps the animal to swim swiftly through the water. A smaller, secondary crest, made up entirely of scales, runs along the base of the tail to the neck.

INTERESTING FACTS

• The Sail-fin Lizard also is known as "water dragon."

• It is a descendant of the bird-hipped dinosaur.

• This lizard can climb trees.

• It blends in well with its environment.

ESTIMATED REMAINING POPULATION

Unknown

REASONS FOR ENDANGERMENT

Although the Sail-fin Lizard's natural predators include rats, water snakes, mongooses, and birds of prey, it also is hunted by people. The lizard is slow-moving on land and has little fear of humans. Thus, it has always been hunted by the islands' natives, whose diet is based on its firm, white meat. The Sail-fin Lizard also suffers from a loss of habitat on the most developed and populated islands.

▶ CONSERVATION MEASURES

Although no special efforts are being made to protect this reptile, it may be possible to maintain a natural population of the Sail-Fin Lizard in reserves on some of the islands.

The male Sail-fin Lizard has a crest along its tail.

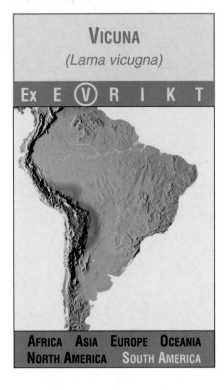

VICUNA
(Lama vicugna)

Ex E Ⓥ R I K T

AFRICA   ASIA   EUROPE   OCEANIA
NORTH AMERICA   SOUTH AMERICA

▶ **DESCRIPTION**

The Vicuna resembles a tall, big-eared, long-necked sheep. Its head, neck, trunk, and thighs are covered with reddish brown wool. A hoofed animal, it is an excellent climber and can easily withstand high altitudes.

▶ **RELATED SPECIES**

Like the Llama and the Alpaca, the Vicuna is a member of the camel family. This animal is the smallest representative of the *Camelidae*.

The Vicuna often is bred for its thick, woolly coat.

SIZE

- Height at the withers: about 3½ feet

- Length: about 5 feet

- Weight: about 110 pounds

HABITAT

The Vicuna inhabits the Andes Mountains, in Peru, Bolivia, and Argentina. This environment is very dry and rocky and tends to be hot during the day and cold at night. The Vicuna climbs to very high altitudes of over 13,000 feet, especially in the summer when the pastures offer large quantities of food. It has a great capacity in its blood to store oxygen. This helps the animal to breathe in its high-altitude habitat.

DIET

This animal feeds on roots, grass, lichens, and moss.

BREEDING AND THE YOUNG

The reproduction period of the Vicuna is between April and June. The gestation period lasts about 10 months. Young that are born at the beginning of the dry season often die due to the shortage of food and water.

THE WOOL

The Vicuna is highly valued because of its wool. It often is bred for its woolly coat, which can be shorn regularly and grown back like sheep's wool. The thick wool helps to keep the animal warm in its mountainous environment.

INTERESTING FACTS

- Each of the Vicuna's feet has two toes.

- Fossil remains indicate that this animal once was found in the vast grasslands of South America.

- It can be crossbred with the Alpaca. This hybrid produces a very valuable, prized wool.

ESTIMATED REMAINING POPULATION

The number of existing Vicunas is not known, but experts say this animal is in danger of extinction.

REASONS FOR ENDANGERMENT

In ancient South American cultures, hunting of this animal was prohibited. The shearing of wool was practiced only during periods established by authorities. After being shorn, the animals were set free in order to assure a continuous supply of wool. More recently, however, the Vicuna has fallen prey to indiscriminate hunting by people who have killed the animal for its wool and then taken its meat. Only in the last century have the governments of countries in which this animal lives taken serious measures for its protection. But even today, local populations hunt the Vicuna for personal use and to sell the wool to tourists.

CONSERVATION MEASURES

Reserves have been established for the protection of the Vicuna in the national park of Sajama in Bolivia, and Cutervo in Peru.

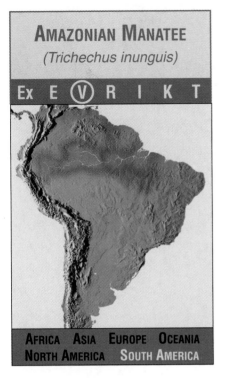

AMAZONIAN MANATEE
(Trichechus inunguis)

Ex E Ⓥ R I K T

AFRICA ASIA EUROPE OCEANIA
NORTH AMERICA SOUTH AMERICA

▶ DESCRIPTION

The Amazonian Manatee has a heavy, fishlike body that ends in a large, flattened fin. It is a gentle, sluggish animal that spends its life in the water. Its thick skin is dark gray and is covered by fine, colorless, almost indistinguishable hairs. Its belly may have one or many white spots. The manatee has five or six functional teeth in each jaw. These are replaced as old teeth fall out.

▶ RELATED SPECIES

The Amazonian Manatee is the smallest of three species of manatee.

▶ SIZE

• Length: up to 9 feet

The Amazonian Manatee has a gentle, affectionate nature.

▶ HABITAT

The Amazonian Manatee lives in the fresh water of lakes and rivers in which the plants to feed on are abundant. It prefers the sheltered waters of the Amazon River, and particularly likes stagnant waters. This animal's current distribution is not known, though it is believed to still exist in one area of Colombia, and may still survive in some restricted areas in Venezuela, Peru, and Brazil.

63

DIET

The Amazonian Manatee eats mainly aquatic plants, although it sometimes eats fruits and vegetables that fall into the water.

BREEDING AND THE YOUNG

Although biological data is scarce, it is believed that this manatee mates at any time during the year, and gives birth to one offspring. The gestation period lasts about one year. The offspring weighs 27 to 31 pounds at birth.

GROUPS

The manatee is a social animal and at one time formed huge groups. Today, only in areas where food is abundant can a group of about four to eight manatees be observed.

INTERESTING FACTS

• The Amazonian Manatee has a mild disposition and an affectionate nature.

• Individual manatees like to playfully rub against one another.

• This animal is extremely slow-moving and easy to capture.

ESTIMATED REMAINING POPULATION

A numerical estimate is not known; however, the Amazonian Manatee is believed to be near extinction, and in some areas has completely disappeared.

REASONS FOR ENDANGERMENT

The Amazonian Manatee has declined in numbers due to uncontrolled hunting. In the 1930s and 1940s, it was hunted at a rate of 7,000 individuals a year. It is estimated that between 1780 and 1962, an average of several thousand animals a year were captured. Apart from being killed for food, the manatee also was wanted for its strong skin, which was used to construct seat belts for cars and containers for water. The manatee has been captured using nets and harpoons and killed by barbaric measures. For example, it sometimes is suffocated by covering its nasal passages so that it cannot breathe.

CONSERVATION MEASURES

The Amazonian Manatee is protected in Peru and Brazil, but it is difficult for the local governments to enforce the laws. Fortunately, however, the manatee's area of distribution is partially included in the National Reserve of Paxaya, in Peru. This manatee is protected by the CITES (Convention on International Trade in Endangered Species) treaty, which prohibits its capture.

CENTRAL AMERICAN MANATEE
(Trichechus manatus)

Ex E (V) R I K T

AFRICA ASIA EUROPE OCEANIA
NORTH AMERICA SOUTH AMERICA

DESCRIPTION

The Central American Manatee is a massive, slow-moving sea mammal. Its round body ends in a large, horizontal tail. Its gray skin is thick and wrinkled. The hairs around the manatee's well-developed mouth are bristly and long, while the rest of the body is covered with short, fine hairs.

RELATED SPECIES

The Central American Manatee is perhaps the most well-known of the three existing species of manatee. This is probably because it lives in areas that are more frequently visited by humans.

SIZE

• Length: 10 to 13 feet

• Weight: up to 1,100 pounds

HABITAT

This species is found in the Atlantic waters of North and South America from Florida to Brazil, including the Caribbean Islands. It also has been seen in Mexico. It prefers warm, coastal waters and inland rivers and estuaries.

DIET

This manatee is basically a herbivore and feeds on all vegetables that grow in the deep waters or on the outskirts of the surface. It searches for food at depths of 3 to 10 feet, using its large upper lip to pick the vegetation it wants to eat.

BREEDING AND THE YOUNG

Mating can occur at any point in the year. The female Central American Manatee gives birth to one offspring after a pregnancy of about a year. The newborn is a grayish black color, but becomes light gray or brown as it grows. It measures a little more than 3 feet at birth and is suckled under the water by the female. It quickly learns to find food on its own. The young manatee stays close to its parents during the first year.

GROUPS

This manatee forms groups of up to six individuals, which do not stay together for long periods of time. The adults and the offspring are very playful with one another.

THE SKIN

The Central American Manatee sheds its thick skin frequently. Because of this, the surface of its body is sprinkled with darker stains in areas where new skin is growing in. The skin might also display deep grooves and scars that are caused by the animal's rubbing against hard objects in deep waters.

MOVEMENT

This manatee moves vertically with its large tail, reaching a speed of about 6 miles per hour. The side fins are of little use to the adult manatee, though the young use these fins to swim while learning to correctly use the tail fin.

INTERESTING FACTS

- It also is known as the Caribbean Manatee.

- This manatee lives in fresh and salt water.

- It has five or six teeth in each jaw that are replaced as old teeth fall out.

ESTIMATED REMAINING POPULATION

An overall estimate of the Central American Manatee population is not known. However, experts believe that at least 1,000 individuals exist in Florida.

The manatee uses its large upper lip to eat aquatic plants.

▶ REASONS FOR ENDANGERMENT

The Central American Manatee population has been severely reduced, mostly because of hunting. The animal has been hunted for its meat, its skin, and its bones. A large, slow-moving animal, it is easy prey for hunters and, more recently, to the blades of passing motor boats. Once very widespread in Central America, this manatee has disappeared from many of its previous distribution areas.

▶ CONSERVATION MEASURES

The Central American Manatee is protected in every major area where it is present. In many areas, however, it is difficult to enforce these laws and it is believed that the animal is still being captured. Today, a few groups of manatees are protected in national parks in the United States, Guatemala, and Costa Rica. The manatee also is protected by the CITES (Convention on International Trade in Endangered Species) treaty.

The Central American Manatee uses its large tail to swim through the water.

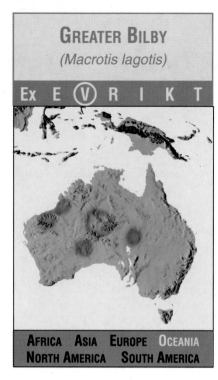

GREATER BILBY
(Macrotis lagotis)

Ex E (V) R I K T

AFRICA ASIA EUROPE OCEANIA
NORTH AMERICA SOUTH AMERICA

▷ **DESCRIPTION**

The Greater Bilby is a small, furry animal with a pointed snout and large, pink ears similar to those of a rabbit. Its fur is a bluish gray color, while its tail is white and black with a striking crest of hairs that it raises high like a flag. This bilby is a fast, agile animal, and it is an excellent digger.

▷ **SIZE**

• Length: 1 to 1½ feet

• Weight: 2 to 3½ pounds

• Length of tail: about 10 inches

▷ **HABITAT**

The Greater Bilby lives on the Australian savanna, a semidesert area with sandy, clay terrain and a few shrubs. Territory inhabited by this bilby is easily recognized because it is usually marked by many holes, about 4 inches deep, distributed everywhere.

The Greater Bilby's ears are similar to those of a rabbit.

DIET
It eats mostly termites and roots, which it digs from the ground with its sharp claws. This animal drinks very little, receiving the water it needs from its food.

THE BURROW
The Greater Bilby is known for its great ability to dig burrows. One type of burrow it creates has a circling or spiral structure that extends 3½ feet into the ground. A second type is more complex, with many entrances connected by a series of tunnels. Usually, the bilby remains all day in its burrow and goes out only at dusk to search for food.

BREEDING AND THE YOUNG
The Greater Bilby constructs a nest out of soft ground. The pregnancy lasts from March to May, and the female gives birth to two offspring. The newborns remain in a pouch located on the mother's back for about 75 days. Afterwards, the bilby keeps the young in its own nest for about two weeks. During this time, the female returns to the nest each night to nurse her offspring.

INTERESTING FACTS
- This animal has poor eyesight, but excellent senses of hearing and smell.

- The Greater Bilby sets aside an area in its burrow to be used as a latrine.

- This animal was considered numerous and well distributed in Australia until the last century.

- The Greater Bilby has disappeared from most parts of Australia.

ESTIMATED REMAINING POPULATION
An accurate estimate of the Greater Bilby population is not known, but experts say this animal is in danger of extinction.

REASONS FOR ENDANGERMENT
The reasons for this species' huge decrease in number are not entirely known. Among the possibilities is the fact that it was hunted pitilessly for its fur and for sport. It also was preyed upon by foxes, and has been forced to compete with rabbits for food and living space.

CONSERVATION MEASURES
No measures are in effect to protect the Greater Bilby from becoming extinct.

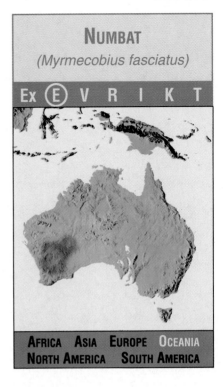

NUMBAT
(Myrmecobius fasciatus)

Ex E V R I K T

AFRICA ASIA EUROPE OCEANIA
NORTH AMERICA SOUTH AMERICA

DESCRIPTION
The Numbat is a small, short-legged animal with a pointed snout and short ears. Its bristly, grayish brown fur is decorated with a series of white, ringlike stripes. Its slender and tapered snout ends with a small oral opening, and its tail ends with a tuft of long hairs that form a kind of plume. The Numbat has a long tongue for eating termites and other insects. It has 52 teeth, all different from one another in shape and strength.

SIZE
- Length: 8 to 10 inches

- Weight: 9½ to 16 ounces

- Length of tail: about 6 inches

*The Numbat spends most of its time
searching for ants and termites to eat.*

▶ HABITAT

The Numbat lives in the wooded areas of Australia.

▶ DIET

The Numbat prefers a solitary life, spending most of its time searching for food. It mainly eats termites and ants, though it occasionally feeds on other small animals. In captivity, a Numbat eats an average of 10,000 to 20,000 termites per day. It eats the small termites whole and chews the larger ones.

▶ BREEDING AND THE YOUNG

The period of reproduction occurs between June and July. The female usually gives birth to a litter of four. The young, which are helpless and not fully developed, immediately attach themselves to the mother and are protected by the heat of the mother's coat.

▶ MARSUPIAL PHASE

Unlike most marsupials, the Numbat does not have a true pouch. For a period of six months, however, the young are constantly attached to the mother, even when she is moving. After this marsupial phase, the mother places the young into a tree cavity or hole in the ground, which serves as a nest. Because the young are unable to move and are easy prey for predators, the mother never strays far away from them.

▶ RESPONSE TO DANGER

The Numbat seems to have two different responses when frightened. When it is confident, it leans on its rear limbs and raises itself in an erect position, showing a clear control of the situation. When it is less sure of itself, the Numbat flattens itself on the ground, ruffling its tail. Then, at the right moment, it flees quickly to a tree cavity. If captured, it almost never bites, but instead makes puffing and whistling sounds.

▶ INTERESTING FACTS

- Unlike most other marsupials, the Numbat is active primarily during the day.

- It takes shelter in tree trunks at night.

- It is quite agile and an excellent tree climber.

- The Numbat's tongue is almost half the length of its body.

▶ ESTIMATED REMAINING POPULATION

The number of existing Numbats is not known, but experts say the animal is in danger of extinction.

▶ REASONS FOR ENDANGERMENT

The destruction of habitat, including the burning and cutting down of trees to make room for agriculture, is the main cause of this animal's endangerment. The Numbat also has fallen prey to a number of animals such as dogs, cats, and foxes that have been introduced to its territory.

▶ CONSERVATION MEASURES

Fortunately, the Numbat's distribution area falls within several nature reserves. In such zones, this animal is protected by law. The entrances to the reserves are guarded by police.

The Bridled Wallaby uses its tail for balance and to rest on.

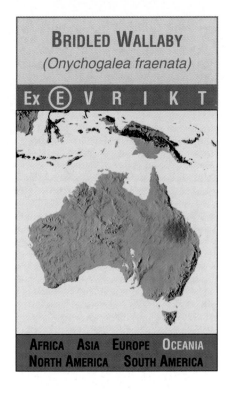

BRIDLED WALLABY
(Onychogalea fraenata)

Ex Ⓔ V R I K T

AFRICA ASIA EUROPE OCEANIA
NORTH AMERICA SOUTH AMERICA

▶ DESCRIPTION

The Bridled Wallaby is a small kangaroo with small front limbs, large, powerful back legs, pointed ears, and a long tail that it uses for balance. It takes its name from the two white fringes, or bridles, that extend from the neck to the elbows on either side of its head. The Wallaby's color is mostly gray with darker stripes.

▶ SIZE

• Length: 1½ to 2 feet

• Weight: about 11 pounds

• Length of tail: 1 to 1½ feet

▶ HABITAT

The Bridled Wallaby inhabits the grasslands of Australia.

Diet

Its diet consists of roots and plants. It particularly likes dry grass.

Breeding and The Young

The female Bridled Wallaby has one litter a year, usually in May. The young live in the mother's pouch for some time before they are ready to go out on their own.

Groups

The Bridled Wallaby is a solitary animal, although at times females and offspring form groups of five or six animals. During the dry season, the wallaby may form much larger groups.

Jumping Ability

Like the kangaroo, the Bridled Wallaby is an excellent jumper. It uses its tail for balance and to help push itself into the air. When it hops, it moves and rotates its arms.

Daily Routine

The Bridled Wallaby is active mostly at night and during twilight. During the day, it stays hidden in the thickets and behind trunks of trees surrounded by leaves.

Response to Danger

The Bridled Wallaby displays some interesting forms of defense. Before it can see danger, it runs with great agility and finds refuge within the bushes. Others run at great speeds and climb to a safe altitude. The Bridled Wallaby becomes almost invisible when it hides among the trees.

Interesting Facts

• The Bridled Wallaby's tail ends with something similar to a claw, the function of which is not clear.

• The wallaby leans on its tail when resting.

• This animal's back paws face forward, unlike those of most wallabies.

Estimated Remaining Population

Unknown

Reasons for Endangerment

Until the beginning of the 20th century, the Bridled Wallaby lived in Australia in great numbers. It suffered a rapid decline because of colonization. The main factors involved in this decline were the loss of habitat to grazing domestic animals, indirect competition for food with the livestock, and the introduction of predatory mammals brought by the colonists.

Conservation Measures

None

NORTHERN HAIRY-NOSED WOMBAT
(Lasiorhinus krefftii)

Ex (E) V R I K T

AFRICA ASIA EUROPE OCEANIA
NORTH AMERICA SOUTH AMERICA

▶ DESCRIPTION

The Northern Hairy-nosed Wombat derives its name from its snout, which is covered by a short, thick, brownish gray colored down. It has a large head and pointy ears that have tufts of white hair at the tips. The wombat has a short tail and legs and walks with a shuffling gait. Its fur is fairly long, very soft, and is a brown color stained with shades of gray.

▶ RELATED SPECIES

This animal is related to the Koala but has characteristics similar to rodents.

▶ SIZE

- Length of body: about 3 to 3½ feet

- Length of tail: about 2 inches

- Length of ears: about 2½ inches

The Northern Hairy-nosed Wombat is given complete protection in the Yepoon Forest, the one place in the world where it lives.

HABITAT

Today, the Northern Hairy-nosed Wombat lives only in the Yepoon Forest in Queensland, Australia. This habitat is a grassland area, populated by eucalyptus and acacia trees.

DIET

The wombat feeds on leaves, grass, roots, sprouts, and bark. It usually searches for food at dusk.

THE BURROW

The Northern Hairy-nosed Wombat is an especially good digger and its burrows can be as deep as one foot. The burrows are isolated or joined in groups of three or four at a time. The tunnels of these burrows are so large that a human baby could crawl through them.

THE YOUNG

The female has a pouch located near her rear. Between January and July, usually one offspring is born. The young wombat lives in the pouch until December.

ELUSIVENESS

The Northern Hairy-nosed Wombat is timid and solitary in nature. It is difficult to observe in nature, especially because it is active only at night and never strays very far away from its burrow. It leaves few traces of where it has traveled.

INTERESTING FACTS

- The wombat can gnaw like a beaver and has the ability to knock down trees by gnawing at the base of the trunk.

- This animal was discovered in 1869 with the finding of a fossilized skull.

- The Northern Hairy-nosed Wombat has very thick fur.

- It is in extreme danger of extinction because its numbers are so low.

ESTIMATED REMAINING POPULATION

A population of fewer than 40 individuals survives in the Yepoon Forest.

REASONS FOR ENDANGERMENT

It is probable that this wombat was numerous only in ancient times and already had become rare by the time of the colonization of Australia. Hunting by both aborigines and colonists further reduced its numbers. The Northern Hairy-nosed Wombat was hunted for its meat, which was considered edible although it had a vague musky taste. The wombat also was hunted because its burrows damaged cultivated areas. Furthermore, rabbits that were brought to the area by the colonists began to crowd out the wombat by taking shelter in its burrows. When the rabbits became so numerous that they constituted a national plague, the inhabitants tried to exterminate them by burning burrows and laying poison. In the process, they also eliminated the Northern Hairy-nosed Wombat.

CONSERVATION MEASURES

The Northern Hairy-nosed Wombat is given complete protection in the Yepoon Forest, the one place in the world where it lives. This area is within an enclosure that does not allow the entry of domestic animals.

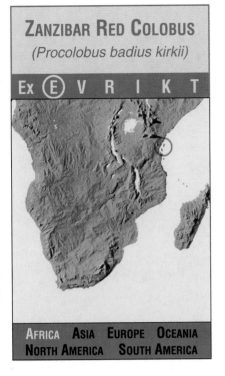

ZANZIBAR RED COLOBUS
(Procolobus badius kirkii)

Ex (E) V R I K T

AFRICA ASIA EUROPE OCEANIA
NORTH AMERICA SOUTH AMERICA

DESCRIPTION
The Zanzibar Red Colobus is distinguished from other monkeys by its tricolored coat. Its long fur is black on the shoulders and forelimbs, chestnut colored on the back, and white on the lower parts of the body and the rear limbs. This monkey has a large tuft of white hair on its forehead.

RELATED SPECIES
It is a monkey belonging to the *bay colobus* group.

HABITAT
This monkey lives on Zanzibar, an island that belongs to the African country of Tanzania. It inhabits the swampy forests and wooded areas of the island.

The Zanzibar Red Colobus has an unusual tricolored coat.

INTERESTING FACTS
• This monkey has a flat, rather humanlike face.

• Its hands and feet are highly developed.

• It spends much of its time in trees.

REASONS FOR ENDANGERMENT
The Zanzibar Red Colobus is endangered because of the continuous destruction of its natural habitat.

ESTIMATED REMAINING POPULATION
Unknown

CONSERVATION MEASURES
The Zanzibar Red Colobus is extremely well protected within Zanzibar's Jozani Forest, which has been a reserve since 1960. A group of the species also was successfully introduced onto the nearby island of Pemba, which is located northeast of Zanzibar.

DRILL
(Papio leucophaeus)

Ex Ⓔ V R I K T

AFRICA   ASIA   EUROPE   OCEANIA
NORTH AMERICA   SOUTH AMERICA

▶ DESCRIPTION

The Drill is a powerful, ground-dwelling baboon. Its eyes are closely set together under heavy brows, and its muzzle is long and heavy. It has strong jaws and sharp, tusklike upper canine teeth. Its coat is mostly brownish gray in color with a deep blue backside. Its beard is white, and its face is black.

▶ RELATED SPECIES

The Drill belongs to the baboon family of monkeys. The four species of baboons are the Sacred Baboon, the Lion Baboon, the Mandrill, and the Drill.

▶ SIZE

- Average length: 2 to 2½ feet

- Weight: about 66 pounds

▶ HABITAT

This baboon lives in Cameroon, an African country near the Sanaga River. It inhabits the primary rain forests and the coastal forests in swampy regions. It prefers clearings where the vegetation is not too thick.

▶ DIET

The Drill eats a variety of foods including fruits, seeds, tubers, roots, mollusks, insects, and small vertebrates. It has a huge appetite.

▶ LIFE ON THE GROUND

Unlike most monkeys, baboons live on the ground instead of in trees. Only the infants and younger animals are good climbers. The adult Drill may occasionally climb a tree, but spends most of its time on the ground.

▶ AGGRESSIVE BEHAVIOR

The Drill is known as an aggressive animal. Its temperament helps it to survive on the ground, where it is likely to meet up with many predators.

▶ GROUPS

The Drill forms groups of about 20 individuals, guided by a single adult male. These groups can sometimes come together to form colonies of up to 200 animals.

▶ INTERESTING FACTS

- Baboons are known as "dog-headed" monkeys.

- The Drill is a fierce fighter.

- It has a highly developed social structure.

- The young Drill can climb up to 23 feet high in a tree.

▶ ESTIMATED REMAINING POPULATION

Unknown

▶ REASONS FOR ENDANGERMENT

The principal reasons for the decline in this species' population are the reduction in habitat due to continual deforestation, and hunting. The Drill was, and still is, hunted for its meat. It also has been killed by farmers because it sometimes raids plantations for food.

▶ CONSERVATION MEASURES

Very few measures have been taken in Cameroon for protecting the Drill, and it is still being hunted. This animal exists in several forest reserves, most notably in Korup, located in southwestern Cameroon. It also is protected by the CITES (Convention on International Trade in Endangered Species) treaty.

The Drill's white beard stands out on its dark face.

JAVAN GIBBON
(Hylobates moloch)

Ex Ⓔ V R I K T

AFRICA **ASIA** EUROPE OCEANIA
NORTH AMERICA SOUTH AMERICA

DESCRIPTION
The Javan Gibbon is a small ape with no tail. Its head is rounded and small with widely set nostrils. The face is black, and its body hair is silvery gray or brown. The edge of the face takes on a whitish coloring. The gibbon uses its extremely long arms to swing among trees with great speed and agility.

SIZE
- Length: about 1½ feet
- Weight: 13 to 15 pounds

HABITAT
This gibbon lives only on the island of Java, in Indonesia. Its inhabits tropical rain forests, highlands, and hilly areas.

THE YOUNG
The gestation period of the Javan Gibbon lasts about seven months, after which a single offspring is born. The baby immediately is cared for and carried around attached to its mother's belly.

MOVEMENT
Using its strong arms and agile hands, which grip objects easily, the gibbon makes skillful leaps from tree to tree within the forest. It is extremely good at flinging itself from one branch to another, hanging from its arms, and gripping branches tightly with its long fingers. This form of movement is known as brachiation. When on the ground, the gibbon usually walks in an upright position with its long arms held wide to balance itself.

INTERESTING FACTS
- The Javan Gibbon uses its hands as a cup from which to drink water.
- It also is known as the Silvery Gibbon.
- This animal often is illegally captured at a young age to be kept as a pet.

REASONS FOR ENDANGERMENT
The causes of the Javan Gibbon's numerical decline are the enormous increase in the human population and the continual, indiscriminate deforestation in the areas where it lives. Because of the exportation of timber, almost all of the forested areas on Java have been cut down. The forest habitats suitable for this ape make up only 7% of the entire island.

ESTIMATED REMAINING POPULATION
The Javan Gibbon is threatened with extinction. The largest colony seems to be in the Gunung Honje Nature Reserve, where the population consists of about 500 animals.

CONSERVATION MEASURES
The Javan Gibbon is protected by the CITES (Convention on International Trade in Endangered Species) treaty. It is legally protected in Indonesia, but the protective laws are difficult to enforce. The species is still captured to be kept by humans as pets.

Because of its coloring, the Javan Gibbon also is known as the Silvery Gibbon.

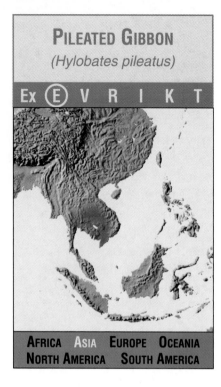

PILEATED GIBBON
(Hylobates pileatus)

Ex **E** V R I K T

AFRICA **ASIA** EUROPE OCEANIA
NORTH AMERICA SOUTH AMERICA

DESCRIPTION
The Pileated Gibbon has thick, silky fur that usually is brown. The hands, feet, eyebrows, and band around the head are lighter in color. This animal has a small round head and a hairless black face surrounded by a sort of beard. Like other gibbons, it has no tail and its arms are extremely long.

SIZE
• Length: 1½ to 2 feet

HABITAT
The Pileated Gibbon is a forest animal that can be found in Laos, Cambodia, and Thailand. It generally inhabits evergreen or deciduous forests, but also has been seen in tropical forests and mountainous regions in Thailand.

THE YOUNG
After a gestation period of about seven months, the female gives birth to a single offspring. The newborn is lovingly cared for by its mother, who carries it about gripped to her belly.

MOVEMENT
This species makes the most of its long, powerful arms to perform long jumps between trees. When on the ground, it assumes an upright position and moves easily, swinging its body from side to side and keeping its arms extended for balance. If it must run on the ground, the gibbon uses its long upper limbs as crutches.

GROUPS
The Pileated Gibbon lives in small family groups generally formed of one male, one or two females, and several young. The young remain with the group until they are 6 or 7 years old.

INTERESTING FACTS
• The Pileated Gibbon already is extinct in Vietnam.

• This animal has very long canine teeth.

ESTIMATED REMAINING POPULATION
The current number of living specimens is not known, but the Pileated Gibbon is surely in decline. In 1977, scientific research established that between 1,300 and 3,000 specimens were present in the Khao Yai National Park, and not more than 500 to 1,500 individuals inhabited the Khao Sol Dao Sanctuary, both located in Thailand. No information is available on the distribution of the Pileated Gibbon in Laos or Cambodia.

REASONS FOR ENDANGERMENT
Deforestation of the Pileated Gibbon's natural habitat is the main reason for its decline. Local inhabitants have cut down the forests to make space for cultivating crops, for building roads, and for constructing dams. In addition, the females of this species are killed for meat, and the young are captured and sold as pets.

CONSERVATION MEASURES
The national park and sanctuary listed above (see *Estimated Remaining Population*) are the only areas in which the Pileated Gibbon is protected. It is protected by CITES (Convention on International Trade in Endangered Species), and killing, possession, sale, and exportation of this species are forbidden in Thailand. With the exception of the protected areas, poaching is frequent is all other areas.

The Pileated Gibbon uses its long, powerful arms to make long jumps between trees.

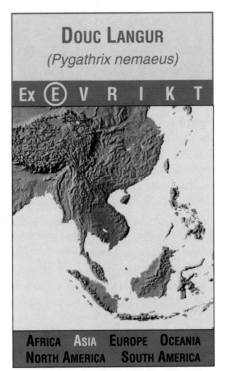

DOUC LANGUR
(Pygathrix nemaeus)

Ex (E) V R I K T

AFRICA **ASIA** EUROPE OCEANIA
NORTH AMERICA SOUTH AMERICA

▶ DESCRIPTION

The Douc Langur is a medium- to large-sized monkey with an unusual coat. Its fur is a contrast between light and dark parts that make the animal look as if it is wearing a shirt and shorts. The color is mostly blackish gray, but the forearms are white, and the legs, from the knee down, are chestnut brown. The hands and feet are completely black, and the tail is white. The cheeks have long, white side whiskers. A collar of reddish brown fur is evident around the neck, and a band of the same color crosses the forehead. The female langur is generally smaller than the male.

The Douc Langur inhabits the tropical rain forests of the Indochinese peninsula.

▶ RELATED SPECIES

Although it is a member of the langur genus, the Douc Langur seems closer in appearance to the snub-nosed monkeys. Two subspecies of Douc Langur are known: *Pygathrix nemaeus nemaeus*, the typical form, and *P.n. nigripes*, which differs in coloring.

▶ SIZE

• Length: 2 to 2½ feet

▶ HABITAT

The tropical rain forests of the Indochinese peninsula are home to the Douc Langur. Its distribution area extends from Laos to Vietnam, and perhaps also into Cambodia.

▶ DIET

The Douc Langur feeds almost entirely on leaves, although it also eats fruit. It rarely drinks because it gets enough water from its diet of fruits and plant substances.

▶ BREEDING HABITS

Although little is known about the reproductive behavior of this species, it appears that the young are born between February and June, probably in relation to the seasonal availability of food and the better climate. Gestation lasts about six months.

▶ INTERESTING FACTS

- The Douc Langur's tail is about the same length as its body.

- This monkey forms regular pathways through the branches of trees.

- It is very agile, can climb quickly, and can leap great distances.

- It eats by raising the food to its mouth with its hands instead of taking it directly with its lips.

▶ ESTIMATED REMAINING POPULATION

A numerical estimation of the population of the Douc Langur is not known, but it appears that the largest population of this animal is in Laos.

▶ REASONS FOR ENDANGERMENT

The wars that have taken place in the Douc Langur's distribution area have contributed greatly to its decline. Warfare brought with it the destruction of the monkey's habitat and, above all, the use of harmful chemical defoliants and bombs. Soldiers also killed the Douc Langur as a form of target practice. Also contributing to this species' decline is hunting by local tribes and the destruction of the forests to accommodate the wood industry.

▶ CONSERVATION MEASURES

In the 1960s, the Douc Langur was protected by the Hanoi government, but the laws had little positive effect. Reserves must be established if the Douc Langur is to survive.

The light-dark coloring of the Douc Langur makes it appear as if it is wearing a shirt and shorts.

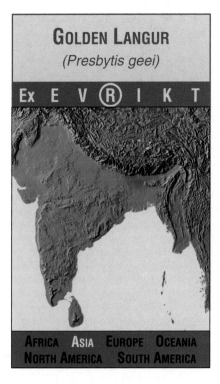

GOLDEN LANGUR
(Presbytis geei)

Ex E V (R) I K T

AFRICA ASIA EUROPE OCEANIA
NORTH AMERICA SOUTH AMERICA

DESCRIPTION

The Golden Langur has a slender body and long tail typical to the langur genus. Its coat varies in color according to the season. The fur is yellowish white in the summer and tends to yellowish brown in the winter. In sharp contrast to its body, the Golden Langur has a black face decorated with a long, pale beard.

SIZE

- Length (male):
  2 to 2½ feet

- Length (female):
  1½ to 2 feet

- Length of tail (male):
  2½ to 3 feet

- Length of tail (female):
  2 to 2½ feet

HABITAT

The Golden Langur inhabits deciduous and evergreen forests that have thick undergrowth. There it lives at altitudes of up to 8,000 feet. Its area of distribution extends from central and eastern Bhutan to the borders of Assam in India, especially between the Sankosh and Manas rivers.

DIET

The langur feeds in the morning and late afternoon. It enjoys a diet of leaves, flowers, and shoots. A tree-dwelling animal, the Golden Langur descends to the ground only to drink from streams.

GROUPS

Golden Langurs live in groups of 10 to 20 individuals, usually guided by an adult male. They do not show rigid territorial behaviors. In fact, the areas between groups often overlap. When a group is disturbed, the females and the young gather together around the adult males, who emit repeated, low-pitched noises.

INTERESTING FACTS

- The Golden Langur is rarely aggressive and avoids meeting humans if possible.

- Langurs also are known as "leaf monkeys."

- The Golden Langur was discovered in 1953.

ESTIMATED REMAINING POPULATION

There are no numerical estimates of the Golden Langur population. It is believed that the animal is not in immediate danger of extinction since it is relatively numerous in Bhutan.

REASONS FOR ENDANGERMENT

Concern for the Golden Langur exists because its area of distribution is so restricted. If the balance of its natural habitat is upset, it could prove harmful to the species.

CONSERVATION MEASURES

The Golden Langur is protected by CITES (Convention on International Trade in Endangered Species) and is completely protected in India. It can be found in a nature reserve in Assam known as the Manas Sanctuary. In Bhutan, the government has declared the region around the Manas River a protected area for the Golden Langur and other animals.

*The Golden Langur lives in groups of 10 to 20 individuals. Its coat
is yellowish white in the summer and yellowish brown in the winter.*